Cambridge Elements Ⲋ

Elements in the Philosophy of Mind
edited by
Keith Frankish
The University of Sheffield

MENTAL CONTENT

Peter Schulte
University of Zurich

Shaftesbury Road, Cambridge CB2 8EA, United Kingdom

One Liberty Plaza, 20th Floor, New York, NY 10006, USA

477 Williamstown Road, Port Melbourne, VIC 3207, Australia

314–321, 3rd Floor, Plot 3, Splendor Forum, Jasola District Centre, New Delhi – 110025, India

103 Penang Road, #05–06/07, Visioncrest Commercial, Singapore 238467

Cambridge University Press is part of Cambridge University Press & Assessment, a department of the University of Cambridge.

We share the University's mission to contribute to society through the pursuit of education, learning and research at the highest international levels of excellence.

www.cambridge.org
Information on this title: www.cambridge.org/9781009217255

DOI: 10.1017/9781009217286

First published 2023

A catalogue record for this publication is available from the British Library.

ISBN 978-1-009-21725-5 Paperback
ISSN 2633-9080 (online)
ISSN 2633-9072 (print)

Mental Content

Elements in the Philosophy of Mind

DOI: 10.1017/9781009217286
First published online: August 2023

Peter Schulte
University of Zurich
Author for correspondence: Peter Schulte, jenspeter.schulte@uzh.ch

Abstract: This Element provides a comprehensive introduction to contemporary theories of mental content. After clarifying central concepts and identifying the questions that dominate the current debate, it presents and discusses the principal accounts of the nature of mental content (or mental representation), which include causal, informational, teleological and structuralist approaches, alongside the phenomenal intentionality approach and the intentional stance theory. Additionally, it examines anti-representationalist accounts that question either the existence or the explanatory relevance of mental content. Finally, the Element concludes by considering some recent developments in the debate about mental content, specifically the "explanatory turn" and its implications for questions about representations in basic cognitive systems and the representational character of current empirical theories of cognition.

Keywords: theories of content, intentionality, mind–body problem, philosophy of cognitive science, mental representation

ISBNs: 9781009217255 (PB), 9781009217286 (OC)
ISSNs: 2633-9080 (online), 2633-9072 (print)

Contents

1 Introduction   1

2 Basic Concepts and Distinctions   2

3 Mental Content: Main Questions   8

4 Theories of Mental Content I: Naturalizing Content   19

5 Theories of Mental Content II: Interpretationism
  and Intentional Stance Theory   43

6 Theories of Mental Content III: The Phenomenal
  Intentionality Approach   47

7 Skepticism about Content: Anti-representationalist
  Approaches   50

8 Recent Developments   55

  References   64

1 Introduction

"Mental content" is a technical term for a very familiar phenomenon. Suppose that Groucho believes that there is money in the safe, Chico hopes that there is money in the safe and Harpo assumes (for the sake of the argument) that there is money in the safe. In this scenario, each Marx brother is in a different mental state: Groucho believes something, Chico hopes something and Harpo assumes something. However, these states are similar in one important respect: what Groucho believes is precisely what Chico hopes and what Harpo assumes. Or, in philosophical terms, the three brothers have different *attitudes* with one and the same *content*.

The fact that we have mental states with content is a crucial fact about our minds. At the same time, it is a fact that is deeply puzzling for at least two reasons. First, a mental state with a content is always *about* or *directed toward* something, usually something in the external world. Groucho's belief that there is money in the safe, for instance, is about the safe and about money being in it. Other beliefs may be about electrons, Alpha Centauri, the library of Alexandria or the tooth fairy. Hence, it seems that a person's mental states can be directed not only toward the proverbial "middle-sized dry goods" in their immediate environment but also toward things that are very small or very far away, things that no longer exist and even things that have never existed at all. This, however, raises the question of what this peculiar relation of "directedness" or "aboutness" is and how it is possible for mental states to stand in that relation to all of these different things.

Secondly, many mental states with content are subject to *semantic evaluation*. Groucho's belief that there is money in the safe can be true or false, depending on whether or not there actually is money in the safe. Similarly, hopes and desires can be fulfilled or unfulfilled, intentions can be realized or not realized and perceptual states can be accurate or inaccurate. These characterizations seem to be *normative* (at least in one sense of this contentious term). But, we may ask, how is it possible for mental states to possess such normative features – especially if we assume, as many contemporary philosophers do, that mental states are ultimately physical in nature?

Moreover, the problems raised by the phenomenon of mental content are more than just intriguing philosophical puzzles. They constitute an important part of what is known as the "mind–body problem," the problem of explaining how our mental characteristics are related to the physical properties of our brains and bodies. Hence, if we can give a convincing account of mental content that explains how human beings (and other animals) are capable of having states that (1) are about things in the world and (2) are subject to standards of truth, realization or accuracy, then we have made a significant step toward solving this age-old philosophical problem.

This Element is about recent philosophical attempts to deal with the phenomenon of mental content. By looking closely at these attempts, we not only learn how contemporary philosophers try to explain (or "explain away") mental content but also gain a better understanding of this multifaceted phenomenon itself and a better appreciation of the many difficulties it poses for the development of a coherent picture of mind in nature.

The Element is structured as follows. In Section 2, I begin by introducing basic concepts and distinctions. In Section 3, I then identify four main questions about mental content that are currently discussed in the literature. The remainder of the Element is devoted to the most central of these questions: the question concerning the nature and reality of mental content. The most prominent naturalistic theories of content are examined in Section 4 and alternative approaches in Sections 5, 6 and 7. Finally, some interesting new developments in the debate about mental content are discussed in Section 8.

2 Basic Concepts and Distinctions

In this section, I will relate the notion of mental content to the cognate notions of intentionality, representation and meaning (Sections 2.1–2.3), draw a distinction between two conceptions of mental content (Section 2.3) and clarify the notion of content further by distinguishing between mental content and phenomenal character (Section 2.4).

2.1 Mental Content and Intentionality

The notion of mental content is very closely related to the notion of *intentionality*, which was reintroduced into the modern debate by the German philosopher and psychologist Franz Brentano. In a famous passage from his book *Psychology from an Empirical Standpoint*, he writes:

> Every mental phenomenon is characterized by what the Scholastics of the Middle Ages called the intentional (or mental) inexistence of an object, and what we might call … reference to a content, direction toward an object … Every mental phenomenon includes something as object within itself, although they do not all do so in the same way. In presentation something is presented, in judgment something is affirmed or denied, in love loved, in hate hated, in desire desired and so on. (Brentano 1874/2009, 88)

It should be noted that it is somewhat controversial what exactly Brentano meant by "intentional (or mental) inexistence" and "direction toward an object" (Crane 1998) and that his ultimate account of intentionality is very different from the one endorsed by most contemporary philosophers (Kriegel 2018). Still, it seems clear that Brentano is concerned with the same phenomenon that I have described in the previous section in terms of mental states being "about" or "directed toward" things in the world, and it is noteworthy that he even uses the term "content" ("Inhalt" in German) to characterize it.

Hence, I submit that the common practice of equating talk of intentionality with talk of mental content is justified.[1] States with content are, *ipso facto*, intentional states, and their content can also be described as their "intentional content."[2]

Brentano is famous not only for drawing the attention of philosophers to the phenomenon of intentionality but also for his claim that intentionality is "the mark of the mental," that is, that all and only mental states are intentional (Brentano 1874/2009, 88). While this strong claim has been attacked from many sides, the weaker thesis that states with intentional content are an essential *ingredient* of minds remains very popular. This reinforces the point made in the previous section that a significant part of answering the mind–body problem consists in developing a satisfactory account of mental content.

2.2 Mental Content and Mental Representation

Another notion that is closely related to the notion of mental content is that of *mental representation*. States with content are often described as representing the world in a certain way: Groucho's belief that there is money in the safe, for instance, is said to represent that a particular safe contains money. Accordingly, contentful states are also called "representational states," or simply "representations," and the term "representational content" is used as (yet another) synonym for "content."

However, there are two important caveats here. First, there is a strong intuitive association between the term "representation" and *belief-like* mental states. It is natural to say that beliefs and perceptual states represent things as being a certain way, but it is less natural to say the same about desires, intentions and suppositions. Hence, when we use the terms "representations" or "representational states" to refer to contentful states in general, we must be clear that these terms do not apply solely to belief-like states. While a subject's beliefs represent how they believe the world to be, their desires represent how they want the

---

[1] By speaking of a "common practice," I do not mean to suggest that equating content with intentionality is wholly uncontroversial (see Section 7 for discussion).

[2] By saying this, I do not mean to imply that all intentional states have *propositional* content, that is, content that can be expressed by a that-clause. There may well be states with irreducibly objectual content (like, e.g., the state of loving a person). For a defense of the claim that not all intentionality can be reduced to propositional ("that-ish") intentionality, see Glock (2015, 515–518).

world to be, their suppositions represent how they suppose the world to be and so on. In short, the term "representational state" in this wider sense applies to contentful states regardless of their attitude type or "psychological mode."

Secondly, "representation" is not always used as a general term for contentful representational states. Often, it is used in a related but significantly different sense: representations in this sense are not complete representational states but constituents or components of such states. Take, for instance, Jerry Fodor's Representational Theory of Mind (RTM) (Fodor 1975, 1987; see also Field 1978). According to RTM, *representations* are mental symbols that have a broadly language-like structure and can thus be described as sentences in a "language of thought" (LOT). A *representational state*, by contrast, is identi-fied with a more complex state of affairs, namely with a subject's standing in a certain type of computational relation to a LOT-sentence. For instance, Jordan's belief that Murnau is the director of "Sunrise" is identified with Jordan's standing in the B-relation (i.e., the computational relation characteris-tic of beliefs) to a LOT-sentence with the content *Murnau is the director of "Sunrise."* What the B-relation is need not concern us here; the important point is that a representation in Fodor's sense (a LOT-sentence) is not identical with but merely a constituent of a full-fledged representational state (a subject's standing in a computational relation to a LOT-sentence).[3]

Furthermore, proponents of RTM usually do not restrict the term "represen-tation" to complete LOT-sentences but apply it also to the concepts of which the LOT-sentences are composed (the "words" of LOT). Hence, it is not only the LOT-sentence MURNAU IS THE DIRECTOR OF "SUNRISE" that qualifies as a representation but also the concepts MURNAU and DIRECTOR.[4]

I will use the term "representation" in a very liberal way in the following, as a term that applies to representational states as well as to mental symbols and their components. However, I will take care to clarify which mental entities I am referring to in contexts where this is necessary.

2.3 Meaning and Two Conceptions of Mental Content

The content of a mental state is also regularly characterized as the state's *meaning* (its *semantic* content).[5] The idea here is that there is a strong analogy

---

[3] Cummins (1996) also distinguishes sharply between representations on the one hand and "atti-tudes" (what I call representational states) on the other. Unlike Fodor, however, Cummins does not hold that an attitude "inherits" its content from the representation it contains as a constituent. According to Cummins, the content of an attitude is dependent on but different from the content of its constituent representation.

[4] Throughout this Element, expressions in capital letters stand for mental symbols.

[5] See, for example, Dretske (1988, 79–81), Cummins (1989, 10) and Millikan (2004, ix).

between mental states and sentences of natural language: saying that one of Groucho's beliefs has *there is money in the safe* as its content is like saying that the English sentence "there is money in the safe" has *there is money in the safe* as its meaning. In both cases, we are ascribing a semantic property to something that bears the property; the difference is just that the property-bearer is a mental state in the first case and a natural language sentence in the second.

Support for this analogy comes from the fact that sentences, like mental states, are usually "about" or "directed at" things in the world and are also subject to semantic evaluations. Like Groucho's belief, the sentence "there is money in the safe," when uttered in appropriate circumstances, is *about* a particular safe (and about money being in it); and it is true iff there is in fact money in the safe.[6] Of course, it may be the case that sentences have these features only because they stand in specific relations to contentful mental states of their users (e.g., to the communicative intentions of speakers of that language, as proposed by Grice 1957), but this would not undermine the analogy.

Still, there is a caveat. Some authors think that equating content with meaning already suggests a particular *conception* of mental content – namely, a "Fregean" conception (named after Gottlob Frege).[7] This brings us to an important distinction between two different conceptions of mental content that often comes up in the literature. A popular way of framing this distinction is to say that the first, *Fregean conception* construes mental content as "intensional," while the second, *non-Fregean conception* construes it as "referential" (see, e.g., Neander 2017, 14–15). However, this characterization is potentially misleading, so I will mostly refrain from using it.[8]

To understand the distinction between the two conceptions, consider the following example. Diotima, who lives in Greece during the sixth century BC, has a belief B_1 that she would express by saying "Hesperus is made of fire" (in Greek) and a belief B_2 that she would express by saying "Phosphorus is made of fire." (Let us also assume that beliefs contain concepts as constituents, B_1 containing HESPERUS and B_2 containing PHOSPHORUS.) Diotima knows that Hesperus is the brightest star in the evening sky, and that

---

[6] This is a very rough formulation. To make it more precise, we would have to say that it is the particular sentence *token* (the utterance of the sentence) that has these specific truth-conditions and that they are determined by the (standard) meaning of the sentence type together with contextual factors. But since this is not an Element about linguistic meaning, I ignore these complications here.

[7] Fodor and Pylyshyn (2015), for instance, argue in their book *Minds without Meanings* that mental states do not have *Fregean* contents ("meanings"), but they do not deny that mental states have *contents*.

[8] For instance, the characterization may suggest that ascriptions of non-Fregean contents do not create "intensional contexts" (i.e., contexts where co-extensional terms cannot be substituted *salva veritate*). However, this is a mistake, as Neander (2017, 36–38) nicely demonstrates.

Phosphorus is the brightest star in the morning sky, but she is not aware of the fact that the names "Hesperus" and "Phosphorus" refer to one and the same object (the planet Venus). Now the question is: Do Diotima's beliefs B_1 and B_2 have the same content?

According to the non-Fregean conception, the answer is "yes": the two beliefs have the same content because they attribute the same property (being made of fire) to the same object (the planet Venus) and are thus true under exactly the same conditions (namely, iff the planet Venus is made of fire). More generally, we can say that, on this conception, a state's content is given by its satisfaction-conditions, that is, its truth-conditions, realization-conditions or accuracy-conditions.[9] Two beliefs with the same truth-conditions *ipso facto* have the same content; and the same holds for two desires with the same realization-conditions and two perceptual states with the same accuracy-conditions. Hence, on the non-Fregean conception, we can characterize mental content not only as "referential" but also as "truth-conditional" (or, more accurately, as "satisfaction-conditional").

Proponents of the Fregean conception, by contrast, hold that Diotima's beliefs B_1 and B_2 have different contents. They agree that B_1 and B_2 attribute the same property to the same object but point to the fact that *the way* the object (Venus) is represented by B_1 and B_2, the "mode of presentation" associated with HESPERUS in B_1 and PHOSPHORUS in B_2, is different – a fact that is reflected in the different cognitive roles that B_1 and B_2 play. According to the Fregeans, this difference should be captured by ascribing different contents or "senses" to the concepts HESPERUS and PHOSPHORUS and also, consequently, to the beliefs in which these concepts occur. Owing to the strong link that holds between content and cognitive role on this picture, Fregean content is sometimes also described as "cognitive content" (Segal 2000, 4; Prinz 2002, 6). (Note that the term "concept" is used here in the sense introduced in Section 2.2, in which concepts are mental particulars that serve as the building blocks of beliefs and other propositional attitudes. The term has also been used in a different sense, especially by Fregeans, as I will explain in Section 3.3.)

It is important not to misinterpret these brief descriptions in uncharitable ways. Of course, non-Fregeans acknowledge that the beliefs B_1 and B_2 play different cognitive roles (e.g., that B_1 is in open conflict with the belief that Diotima would express by saying "Hesperus is made of ice," while B_2 is not); they merely think that this difference does not reflect a difference in the *contents*

---

[9] Note that I am using "satisfaction-conditions" as a catchall term for truth-, realization- and accuracy-conditions (following, e.g., Fodor 1985/1990, 5) and not, like some other authors, as a term for the conditions under which a predicate applies to an object (as in "the predicate 'green' is satisfied by x iff x is green").

of B_1 and B_2. Similarly, Fregeans do not deny that beliefs have truth-conditions or that other representational states have other kinds of satisfaction-conditions. Instead, they standardly maintain that a state's satisfaction-conditions are *determined* by its Fregean content (or by its Fregean content together with contextual factors). On this view, satisfaction-conditions are derivative, and the content that is (supposedly) constituted by them is only of a secondary kind.

Given these remarks, it will come as no surprise that, in order to evaluate a theorist's claims about content, it is often of vital importance to clarify which conception of content they have in mind. For this reason, the distinction between Fregean and non-Fregean conceptions of content will come up again in several different contexts, for example in the section on the debate about narrow and broad content (Section 3.2), the section on reified contents (Section 3.3) and several later sections about different theories of mental content.

2.4 The Distinction between Mental Content and Phenomenal Character

Finally, it is important to distinguish the notion of representational content from the notion of *phenomenal character* and to recognize that the relationship between representational and phenomenal properties of mental states is far from straightforward. To understand what phenomenal character is, consider states of mind like being in pain, feeling joy or hearing a loud noise. Intuitively, for each of these states, *there is something it is like* for a subject to be in that state. This "what-it's-like" aspect is called the phenomenal or qualitative character of the state; some theorists also describe it as the state's "quale" (plural: "qualia"). States with phenomenal character are said to be "phenomenally conscious." On a conceptual level, it is clear that we can distinguish a state's phenomenal character from its content. This leads to the controversial issue of how these properties are related to each other.

To investigate it, we can start by asking: Are all states with representational content also states with phenomenal character? First of all, it seems hard to deny that there are *some* mental states with representational content that also have phenomenal character, namely perceptual experiences. If I have a visual experience of (or "as of") a blue triangle, then this state represents the world as being a certain way, and there is also something it is like to be in that state. But, according to most theorists, some other states with representational content *lack* phenomenal character – for example, belief states. On this view, beliefs themselves do not have a specific "what-it's-like" aspect, although they may often be accompanied by other states (e.g., episodes of inner speech) that do have such an aspect. However, there is a significant minority of theorists who reject this position and who maintain that *all* states with (genuine) representational content or (genuine) intentionality must also have phenomenal character (see Section 6 for further discussion).

Let us also briefly consider the reverse question: Do all states with phenomenal character also have representational content? Here, again, opinion is divided. Some theorists hold that there are states with phenomenal character that lack representational content, citing bodily sensations like hunger and pain or moods like elation and sadness as examples (Searle 1983, 1–2; McGinn 1996, 8); others argue that all these states do in fact have a representational content, although it may not be immediately obvious what that content is (Dretske 1995; Tye 1995).

Finally, we can ask about the relationship between the representational content of a state and its phenomenal character, *given* that the state has both of these properties. Is the state's content determined by its phenomenal character or vice versa? Or are these two properties independent of each other? As the formulation of this question already suggests, there are three different theoretical options available here, all of which have in fact been advocated in the literature. Some philosophers contend that phenomenal character is determined by representational content, so that there can be no difference in phenomenal character without a corresponding difference in representational content (Dretske 1995; Tye 1995). This position is called "intentionalism" or "representationalism about phenomenal character" (sometimes also, misleadingly, "representationalism" *tout court*). Other philosophers maintain that it is the other way around: representational content is determined by phenomenal character. Their position is known as the "phenomenal intentionality approach" (see Section 6). Yet other philosophers hold, finally, that phenomenal character and representational content are independent properties of mental states (see, e.g., Papineau 2021).

The main purpose of this subsection is a clarificatory one: by distinguishing between representational content and phenomenal character, we can now see more clearly what this Element is (and is not) about. In addition to that, however, this subsection prepares the ground for the discussion of the phenomenal intentionality approach in Section 6, where we will get back to the question concerning the relationship between these two crucial features of mental states.

3 Mental Content: Main Questions

In this section, I will present the questions concerning mental content that loom large in contemporary philosophy of mind. I will start with the organizing question of this Element, which was already mentioned in the Introduction: the question concerning the nature and reality of content – or, more precisely, the nature and reality of content *properties* (Section 3.1). In addition to this fundamental question, there are several more specific issues concerning mental content that have been discussed extensively by philosophers: the question of whether mental content is narrow or broad, questions concerning the nature of reified contents and the question of whether mental content can be nonconceptual. It is with these issues that the rest of the section is concerned (Sections 3.2–3.4). While they are not at the center of this Element, they are interrelated (in multiple ways) with our central question and thus come up again several times in later sections.

3.1 The Fundamental Issue: The Nature and Reality of Content Properties

Consider, once again, Groucho and his belief that there is money in the safe. In this scenario, Groucho is in a contentful mental state, a state that instantiates the property of having the content *there is money in the safe* (a "content property," in my terminology). Now, the fundamental philosophical question that arises is this: What makes it the case that Groucho is in a state that instantiates such a property? Or, more generally, what is the nature of this property?

To make things more vivid, let us assume that the state instantiating the content property is a brain state, *n*, of Groucho's. (Such a brain state is called a "vehicle" or "vehicle state," since it can be described as "carrying" the content in question.) What we are interested in, then, is the nature of the content property instantiated by *n*. Is it a property that *n* has because it instantiates certain other properties (e.g., physical-functional properties)? Or is it a fundamental property that is incapable of further explanation?

The claim that content properties are fundamental features of reality may be called "content primitivism." Prima facie, this is not a very attractive position and is usually seen only as a last resort if all attempts at explaining content properties fail.[10] Hence, most theorists who are realists about content properties hold the non-primitivist view that these properties can be explained in some way or other. Or, to be more precise, they hold the view that we can give a *constitutive* explanation of content properties, an account of *what makes it the case* that certain brain states instantiate content properties.

There is, however, a deep division among the group of non-primitivist realists. *Semantic naturalists* maintain that content properties can be explained in terms that are purely naturalistic or "naturalistically acceptable." The precise meaning of this "naturalistic proviso" is a matter of controversy, but it is not empty, since (1) it is clear that it excludes explanations of content couched in primitive mental

---

[10] An exception may be Paul Boghossian (1990, 1991), who seems to lean toward a primitivist position.

or normative vocabulary and (2) it is usually interpreted as allowing for explanations that appeal (among other things) to relations of causation, counterfactual dependence, probabilistic dependence and structural similarity.

Other theorists, by contrast, hold that content properties can only be explained in terms that are excluded by the naturalistic proviso. The most prominent among them are the adherents of the *phenomenal intentionality approach* (already mentioned in Section 2.4), who hold that the representational content of a mental state is determined by its phenomenal character.

In addition to the three broad approaches just sketched, there are further theoretical options. One option is to deny that content properties are real and to adopt (what we might call) *content eliminativism*. Most of the time, content eliminativism is only defended as a local thesis about some type of mental state (e.g., about perceptual states or the states of non-linguistic creatures), but some versions of syntacticism and radical enactivism tend toward a global form of the eliminativist view.

A further alternative is proposed by theorists who accept statements about the contents of mental states as true but take an *interpretivist* or *weakly realist* attitude toward them. Contrary to the variants of "robust" or "strong" realism discussed earlier in the section, they hold that content properties are neither primitive features of reality nor capable of being constitutively explained; but contrary to content eliminativism, they maintain that content properties are nevertheless real.

Questions concerning the nature and reality of content properties will take center stage in this Element. A more detailed discussion of the answers presented here, of different ways of spelling them out and of their advantages and problems will be the topic of Sections 4–7.

3.2 Is Mental Content Narrow or Broad (or Both)?

One of the more specific issues concerning content that have been widely discussed is the question of whether mental content is narrow or broad. To put it roughly, the content of a person's mental states is *narrow* if it depends only on what goes on in the person themself and *broad* (or *wide*) if it also depends on what their environment is like. If we presuppose a naturalistic picture of human beings, we can also put the question this way: Is the content of a person's mental states fully determined by the intrinsic properties of their brain and body, or is it also partly determined by their environment?[11]

---

[11] More precisely, the question is whether the content of a person's mental states is fully determined by the intrinsic properties of their brain and body *together with the laws of nature* (see Braddon-Mitchell and Jackson 2007, 242). This qualification is always implicitly presupposed in the following.

To a first approximation, *content externalists* hold that mental content is often broad, while *content internalists* maintain that mental content is always narrow. To forestall misunderstandings, however, two clarifications are in order. First, this debate is not about the *causal* dependence of contentful mental states on the environment. All participants in the debate agree that beliefs, desires and perceptual states are causally influenced by environmental factors. The question is whether the environmental factors are part of what *constitutes* a state's content (what *makes it the case* that the state has this or that particular content).

Secondly, the disagreement between externalists and internalists does not concern the content of the indexical or demonstrative elements of mental representations (elements expressed by terms like "I," "here," "now" and "this"). To see this clearly, consider the following hypothetical case. Alice and Alice* are intrinsic duplicates of each other (i.e., they are exactly the same "from the skin in"). While Alice is in Nauru and Alice* in Tuvalu, they both think "It is sunny here." Now it may seem that internalists are committed to the claim that Alice and Alice* have thoughts with exactly the same content (since they have exactly the same intrinsic properties), while externalists can allow that the contents of their thoughts are different. In fact, however, most internalists adopt a more complex view: they maintain that, while there is a clear sense in which the two thoughts have the same content, there is *also* a sense in which their contents are different. After all, Alice thinks that it is sunny *in Nauru* (a thought that is true iff it is sunny in Nauru), whereas Alice* thinks that it is sunny *in Tuvalu* (a thought that is true iff it is sunny in Tuvalu). Most internalists do not deny that this difference can be described as a difference in content of *some* kind, but they claim that this kind of content is irrelevant to their thesis – for example, because it is a merely derivative form of content (Braddon-Mitchell and Jackson 2007, 254–256) or because it is a type of content that is not genuinely "cognitive" or "psychological" (Segal 2000, 19). In any case, the crucial disagreement between internalists and externalists only emerges when we consider the non-indexical elements of mental representations.

With these clarifications in mind, let us now turn to the debate itself. For much of the twentieth century, realists about mental representations seem to have taken content internalism for granted. This only changed in the 1970s, mainly due to a series of influential thought experiments put forward by Hilary Putnam (1975) and Tyler Burge (1979). These thought experiments were designed to show that both linguistic meaning and mental content are, at least in some cases, broad, that is, dependent on a person's environment.

The most famous of these thought experiments is Putnam's "Twin Earth" scenario, which I will present here in a modified form (adapted from Segal 2000, 6). Suppose that Abigail, who lives on Earth in the seventeenth century, has the true belief that diamonds exist. Now imagine that there is a faraway planet exactly like Earth, except for the fact that the gemstones that look like diamonds and that are used like diamonds by the inhabitants of this planet do not consist of carbon (as diamonds do) but of some kind of aluminum oxide. Let us call this planet "Twin Earth" and the diamond-like gemstones that are found on it "twin diamonds" (although, in the language spoken by twin earthlings, the planet is called "Earth" and the gemstones "diamonds"). Since the microphysical composition of diamonds was completely unknown in the seventeenth century, we can imagine that the history of both planets up to that time is almost exactly alike, too. Finally, let us suppose that there is an intrinsic duplicate of Abigail on Twin Earth (Twin Abigail), who – like Abigail – has a belief that she would express by saying "diamonds exist."

Do the beliefs of Abigail and Twin Abigail have the same content? Intuitively, the answer is "no." Abigail has the (true) belief that *diamonds* exist, while Twin Abigail has the (true) belief that *twin diamonds* exist, and diamonds are different from twin diamonds. (Of course, Abigail and Twin Abigail would not be able to distinguish them, but that does not change the fact that they are minerals of two very different kinds.) However, *ex hypothesi*, Abigail and Twin Abigail are intrinsically exactly alike. Hence, the difference in their belief contents cannot be due to a difference in their intrinsic properties but must be due to the fact that they are situated in different environments. In other words, their belief contents are broad. Or so the externalists argue.

While many philosophers find this argument convincing, proponents of content internalism staunchly resist it. One possible internalist response is to reject the claim that Abigail's and Twin Abigail's beliefs have different contents. Gabriel Segal, for example, argues that, strictly speaking, Abigail does not believe that *diamonds* exist (Segal 2000, 121–126). Segal accepts that *our* DIAMOND concept is a natural kind concept that applies to all and only those things that are made of carbon atoms arranged in a diamond cubic structure, but he holds that *Abigail's* (prescientific) DIAMOND concept is different: it applies to all and only those things that have certain surface features (roughly speaking, to things that are transparent, colorless, shiny and very hard). And exactly the same is true of Twin Abigail's DIAMOND concept. Hence, they both believe the same thing. What they believe is difficult to express in our language, but we can approximate it by saying that they both believe in the existence of *diamond-like things*.

Another option for internalists is to accept that the beliefs of Abigail and Twin Abigail have different contents but to argue that this is due to an implicit indexical element contained in the DIAMOND concepts of both Abigails, so that the word "diamond" in their idiolect is roughly equivalent to "the hard, transparent, shiny minerals that are found *around here*," and is thus able to pick out different minerals on earth and twin earth. This is, in effect, the response given by Frank Jackson (1998, 37–41). On Jackson's view, the difference in content between Abigail's and Twin Abigail's belief is real, but it is only a difference in a derivative or secondary kind of content, and thus not inconsistent with the truth of internalism.[12]

As this discussion makes clear, the internalism/externalism debate is closely connected to the dispute between Fregeans and non-Fregeans examined in Section 2.3. Proponents of a non-Fregean conception of content hold that two states that represent some x as being F count as having the same content iff they attribute the same property F to the same object x. Accordingly, they are (on standard assumptions) committed to the claim that content depends on factors that are external to the representing system, that is, to content externalism.[13] When it comes to the Fregean position, matters are less straightforward. While it is natural for Fregeans to hold that ("cognitive" or primary) content is narrow, and thus to opt for content internalism, this is not mandatory.[14] In short, we can say that non-Fregean content is (virtually) always construed as broad, while Fregean content is usually, but not always, construed as narrow.

The externalism/internalism debate is still ongoing. In addition to the contributions of Putnam and Burge, the work of Saul Kripke (1980) and other proponents of (so-called) causal theories of reference has exerted a major influence on it. Moreover, the debate has recently been reinvigorated by a full-scale attack on the notion of narrow content by Juhani Yli-Vakkuri and John Hawthorne (2018) and by the various responses to this attack. (For an up-to-date overview of this debate, see Brown 2022, sec. 7.)

---

[12] Jackson's theory is a variant of "two-dimensional semantics," or "2D semantics." For a survey, see Nimtz (2017).

[13] The qualifier "on standard assumptions" is necessary because it is theoretically possible to combine a non-Fregean view of content with the following conjunction of claims: (i) all nominative concepts of a subject (i.e., all concepts that refer to individual objects) are indexical, (ii) all predicative concepts of a subject refer to properties that the subject is directly acquainted with, and (iii) intrinsic duplicates are acquainted with exactly the same properties. On this view, non-Fregean contents would qualify as narrow. To be sure, this is a highly unusual position, but it is at least similar to the view defended by Russell (1918/85). (I would like to thank an anonymous reviewer for pointing this out to me.)

[14] Fregeans hold that representational contents are *fine-grained*. They maintain, for instance, that the belief that Hesperus is made of fire and the belief that Phosporus is made of fire possess different contents, despite the fact that these two beliefs attribute the same property to the same object. However, it is open to Fregeans to adopt the view that these fine-grained contents are partly constituted by external factors, and thus to endorse externalism about Fregean content. A well-known proponent of this type of Fregean externalism is Burge (2010).

3.3 Reified Contents: The Nature and Existence of Propositions

Another question that I subsume under the category of "specific issues" concerns the existence and nature of contents, strictly speaking – or, in other words, the existence and nature of contents *as opposed to content properties*. To see that these are two subtly different questions, consider Abbott's belief that cake is nutritious. This belief instantiates the property of having the content that cake is nutritious. But does that mean that the belief stands in a relation of "having" (or "carrying") to something – some entity – that can be called "the content that cake is nutritious"?

Here is a simple argument for an affirmative answer to this question. Suppose that Abbott and Costello both believe that cake is nutritious. Then it seems that *there is something* that they both believe, namely that cake is nutritious. This "something" is a content; therefore, the content that cake is nutritious exists. Proponents of this argument usually add that this content can also be described as a "propositional content," or simply as a "proposition" – namely, the proposition that cake is nutritious (or <cake is nutritious>, for short).

Propositions have long been an important topic in philosophy, especially in the twentieth century. In addition to being treated as the contents of propositional attitudes (i.e., the things that are believed, desired and so on), they have also been described as the primary bearers of truths and falsity (i.e., the things that are true or false in a nonderivative way). But are there really such entities? And if so, what is their nature?

How we answer the first question depends, in part, on our attitude toward the simple argument I have just presented.[15] The first premise of this argument seems unproblematic. Surely, it is often true that two persons believe the same thing, so it may well be true that Abbott and Costello both believe that cake is nutritious. But does it follow from this truism that we are ontologically committed to some *entity* that Abbott and Costello both believe, that is, to some proposition that both subjects are related to by the belief-relation, or (equivalently) that their beliefs are related to by the having-as-content relation? There are several different positions one can take here. First, it is possible to maintain that the statement "there is something (i.e., some proposition) that Abbott and Costello both believe" is, strictly speaking, false, even though it is sometimes useful to talk this way. Secondly, one can argue that the existence claim is true but does not carry ontological commitment to propositions, since the existential quantifier employed in it is a "lightweight" quantifier.[16] Thirdly,

---

[15] Only "in part" because there are also other arguments that can be given for the existence of propositions (see, e.g., McGrath and Frank 2020, sec. 4).

[16] The distinction between "lightweight" and "heavyweight" quantification is due to Chalmers (2009). According to Chalmers, lightweight quantification is existential language of a sort that can be used in existence claims that are trivially (and, perhaps, analytically) true, while heavyweight quantification is existential language that cannot be used in this way (Chalmers

one can accept that the existence claim is true and that it involves "heavyweight" quantification. Only theorists who endorse the third answer are ontologically committed to propositions, and it is only for these theorists that the second question arises, namely what is the nature of these propositions?

Again, there are several options here, the three most prominent being the *Fregean*, the *Russellian* and the *possible worlds approach*. The Fregean approach goes back, once more, to Gottlob Frege (1892/1994a, 1892/1994b). It is closely related to the Fregean conception of content (discussed in Section 2.3) but not identical to it, as we will see in a moment. Proponents of the Fregean approach to propositions hold that propositions are abstract entities that contain other abstract entities as constituents, so that the identity of a proposition is determined by these constituents (together with the way in which they are combined). The proposition expressed by "Fred loves Ginger", for example, contains three constituents corresponding to the words "Fred," "loves" and "Ginger", combined in a specific way. Frege calls these constituents the "senses" of "Fred," "loves" and "Ginger," while contemporary Fregeans usually describe them as the "concepts" expressed by these words (see, e.g., Peacocke 1992).[17] (This is the second sense of "concept" that I alluded to back in Section 2.3 – the "abstract objects sense," as we might call it. Note that concepts in this sense are fundamentally different from concepts in the first, "mental particulars" sense.)

Proponents of the Russellian approach,[18] by contrast, hold that propositions are (or involve) set-theoretic constructions out of ordinary ("worldly") individuals, properties and relations (Salmon 1986; Soames 1987). On a simple version of this view, the proposition expressed by "Fred loves Ginger" can be identified with an ordered pair consisting of (i) the ordered pair of Fred and Ginger and (ii) the loving-relation R_L, that is. with $\ll$Fred, Ginger>, R_L>. (For more sophisticated variants of this approach, see King 2007; Soames 2010.)

Finally, adherents of the possible worlds approach hold that propositions are sets of possible worlds, or complex set-theoretic constructions involving possible worlds (Lewis 1972; Stalnaker 1976). What possible worlds are is a further question, but roughly speaking, they can be thought of as complete ways the world could be. According to the simplest version of the possible worlds approach, the proposition expressed by "Fred loves Ginger" can be identified

---

2009, 95–96). Proponents of other "neo-Carnapian" approaches to meta-ontology draw similar distinctions (see, e.g., Hofweber 2005).

[17] Confusingly, for Frege himself, a concept ("Begriff") is not the sense ("Sinn") of a predicate but its *referent* ("Bedeutung") (Frege 1892/1994b).

[18] This approach is inspired by Bertrand Russell's (1903, 47) *Principles of Mathematics*, although contemporary Russellian accounts differ considerably from the view that Russell sketched in this work.

with the set of all possible worlds where this statement is true, that is, where it is the case that Fred loves Ginger. This is a very coarse-grained conception of propositions (it entails, e.g., that all necessarily true statements express the same proposition, since they are all true in every possible world), but there are also other versions of the possible worlds approach that construe propositions in a more fine-grained way (Lewis 1972; Cresswell 1985).

The debate about the nature and existence of propositions is interesting in itself, but its relationship to the issues that are at the center of this Element is rather indirect. First, we should note that this debate is not connected in a straightforward way to the dispute between proponents of Fregean and non-Fregean conceptions of content. While proponents of both of these camps are (arguably) committed to realism about content properties,[19] this does not mean that they are automatically committed to realism about reified contents (propositions). Instead, they may well adopt the view that quantifying about propositions is just a useful manner of speaking or that it only involves lightweight quantification. Moreover, even if they adopt a realist attitude toward propositions, there is more than one theoretical option open to them. It is true that the Fregean conception of content fits well with a Fregean approach to propositions and is inconsistent with a Russellian approach, and that the reverse holds for the non-Fregean conception of content, but it seems that both conceptions can also be combined with certain versions of the possible worlds approach.

Secondly, for exactly parallel reasons, views concerning the existence and nature of propositions are only indirectly connected to the theories of content that we will examine in the following sections. In general, these theories are concerned with the nature of content properties and are neutral on the existence of propositions; and even if they are combined with realism about propositions, most of them can be combined with several different approaches toward the nature of propositions.

For these reasons, the debate about the nature of propositions (or other kinds of reified contents) will not play a major role in this Element.

3.4 Can Mental Content Be Nonconceptual?

One last issue that we should briefly examine here is the question of whether representational states can have "nonconceptual content." This question has

---

[19] Does this mean that these theorists are committed to reject a radical nominalist view that says that (strictly speaking) properties do not exist? No, it does not. Here is a more careful formulation of the position that they are actually committed to: "if properties exist (strictly speaking), then content properties exist; and if properties do not exist (strictly speaking), then talk of content properties must be treated like talk of mass, charge and speed (which is a kind of property talk that any reasonable version of nominalism must be able to accommodate in some way or other)."

been the topic of much discussion since Gareth Evans introduced the notion of nonconceptual content in *The Varieties of Reference* (1982). Evans and other nonconceptualists claim that there is an important difference between (a) beliefs and other propositional attitudes, which have conceptual content, and (b) other representational states, for example perceptual experiences, which have content that is nonconceptual.

One popular line of thought in support of this claim is this.[20] Suppose that I believe that there is something blue in front of me. On the (Neo-)Fregean account of reified contents sketched in the previous section, the content of this belief is a proposition that consists of concepts. More precisely, it is the proposition *that there is something blue in front of me*, which consists, among other things, of the concept *blue* (where "concept" is to be understood in the "abstract objects sense"; see Section 3.3). Moreover, it is very plausible to suppose that I can have a belief with this content only if I possess the concepts involved (e.g., the concept *blue*).

Now consider the perceptual experience on which my belief is based. Prima facie, it seems clear that this experience does not merely represent the object in front of me as being blue but as having a particular shade of blue (say, $blue_{36}$). However, I do not have the concept $blue_{36}$: I could not, for instance, reidentify something as being $blue_{36}$ just by looking at it. My color concepts are simply not that fine-grained. Hence, the content of my perceptual experience (which *is* that fine-grained) must be nonconceptual.

This argument, known in the literature as the "fineness of grain" argument, has been subjected to various criticisms by opponents of nonconceptual content. John McDowell, for instance, argues that ordinary perceivers do have concepts that are suitably fine-grained to capture the content of perceptual states, namely *demonstrative concepts*, which can be expressed in ordinary language by descriptions like "this shade of blue" (McDowell 1994, 56–57). It is unclear, however, whether this suffices to undermine the fineness of grain argument (for replies to McDowell, see Heck 2000; Kelly 2001; Tye 2006).

This is just one of numerous arguments that are discussed in the debate about nonconceptualism (for a survey, see Bermúdez and Cahen 2020). Instead of delving further into these arguments, however, I will now turn to an important distinction that was introduced by Richard Heck (2000) and that has been a major factor in shaping the current debate on this topic: the distinction between *state* and *content* nonconceptualism.

---

[20] This argument is suggested by Evans (1982, 229) but more fully developed by other authors (see, e.g., Tye 1995, 139; Heck 2000; Tye 2006). For a recent discussion, see Schmidt (2015, 74–97).

Heck points out that the nonconceptualist thesis can be understood in two different ways. First, it can be understood straightforwardly as a thesis about *contents*, that is, as the claim that some representational states have contents that do not consist of concepts and are thus of a fundamentally different kind than the contents of beliefs and other propositional attitudes. A version of this view is defended by Christopher Peacocke (1992, 61–74), who holds that perceptual states have so-called scenario contents.[21] Secondly, nonconceptualism can be interpreted as a thesis that is not really about contents but about the *states* that have the contents. On this interpretation, nonconceptualism is the claim that there are some representational (i.e., contentful) states that are "concept-independent," where this means, roughly speaking, that they can represent something as being F (e.g., as being $blue_{36}$), even though the subject who is in the state does not have the concept F (e.g., the concept $blue_{36}$). Such concept-independent states stand in contrast to beliefs and other propositional attitudes, which appear to be "concept-dependent."[22]

This distinction is highly significant, since it is possible to endorse one of these claims without endorsing the other, or, more generally, to hold either that (i) there are concept-dependent states with non-conceptual content or that (ii) there are concept-independent states with conceptual content. A clear instance of position (i) is provided by proponents of possible worlds semantics who identify contents with sets of possible worlds (see Section 3.3) and are thus committed to the claim that *all* contents, even those of beliefs, are nonconceptual (i.e., do not consist of concepts). Nevertheless, these theorists need not (and typically do not) deny that beliefs are concept-dependent states. An instance of position (ii) is the view, tentatively suggested by some authors, that perceptual states, while concept-independent, still have conceptual contents (see, e.g., Crowther 2006, 255); we should note, however, that the coherence of this position is disputed (Bermúdez 2007).

These considerations make it plain that there is a considerable gap between the thesis of state nonconceptualism and the thesis of content nonconceptualism – a gap that can only be bridged by substantive arguments, if at all. Moreover, they also suggest that much of the debate that is ostensibly about "nonconceptual content" is really about the concept-independence of representational states.

---

[21] Very roughly, the scenario content of a perceptual state is the set of possible "ways of filling the space around the subject" (Peacocke 1992, 62) that would make it the case that the perceptual state in question is correct.

[22] If we accept that there are concepts in the "mental particulars sense" (see Section 2.3), then the distinction between concept-dependent and concept-independent representational states can be analyzed as the distinction between states that contain concepts as constituents and states that do not.

4 Theories of Mental Content I: Naturalizing Content

While I type these words, I have visual experiences of black shapes suddenly appearing in front of a white background. Can we give a constitutive explanation of why it is the case that I have experiences with this content? As we have seen in Section 3.1, semantic naturalists maintain that it is possible (at least in principle) to give such an explanation. Moreover, they hold that this explanation can be couched in purely naturalistic or "naturalistically acceptable" terms, where this excludes appeals to primitive mental or normative notions but allows for an appeal to notions like causation, counterfactual dependence, probabilistic dependence or structural similarity.

Semantic naturalizers are those proponents of semantic naturalism who go one step further and actually try to provide a constitutive explanation of content, either for representational states in general or for a significant subclass of them.[23] Such accounts are usually called "naturalistic theories of content." Furthermore, given that "representational states" is used as a synonym for "states with content" (see Section 2.2), these accounts can also be described as "naturalistic theories of representation."

Naturalistic theories of content/representation aim to answer two basic questions:

(1) What makes it the case that a state R has content at all, rather than no content? (Or, in other words, what makes it the case R qualifies as a representational state?)
(2) What makes it the case that a state R has content p rather than some other content p*, given that R is a representational state?

The first question is known as the *representational status question* (or status question), the second as the *content-determinacy question* (or content question).[24] As we will see, not all theorists try to answer both questions; some focus exclusively on the content question, thus only providing a partial theory of content/representation.

Moreover, as I have already indicated, not all naturalistic theories of content are fully general in scope. Some are restricted to some subclass M of representational states. Hence, they only aim to provide answers to restricted versions of the status question ("what makes it the case that R is a M-representation?") and

---

[23] In doing so, semantic naturalizers adopt the working assumption that naturalistic explanations of content are not only possible in principle but also epistemically accessible to us, given our current knowledge and our limited cognitive capacities. This is an assumption that some semantic naturalists might reject (cf. Loewer 2017, 175).

[24] This specific terminology is due to Neander (2017, 5), but the distinction is found in many authors (see, e.g., Cummins 1989, 10; Sterelny 1995, 254; Artiga 2016, 410).

the content question ("what makes it the case that R has the content p rather than some other content p*, given that R is a M-representation?"). For instance, some theories are restricted to perceptual representations (see Section 4.4) and others to "descriptive" representations.[25]

To clarify this last point, let me briefly explain the notion of a descriptive representation. It has been observed by many theorists that most representational states seem to fall into one of two classes: (i) the class of descriptive, "cognitive" or "belief-like" representations or (ii) the class of directive, "conative" or "desire-like" representations. States of the first class (e.g., beliefs, perceptual representations and the like) are said to have a "mind-to-world direction of fit."[26] The idea here is that such states "aim to fit the world": they are supposed to change in response to changes in the world. States of the second class, on the other hand (e.g., desires, intentions and goals), are characterized as having a "world-to-mind direction of fit": they "aim at making the world fit them." For instance, my belief that my hair is short changes as soon as I notice that my hair is growing longer; my desire to have short hair, by contrast, persists and causes me to go to the barber. This is a very loose account of the difference that leaves many questions open, but it should suffice for our purposes.

Finally, we should note that most semantic naturalizers explicitly or implicitly presuppose a non-Fregean conception of content (see Section 2.3). Consequently, the kind of content their theories aim to explain is non-Fregean, "referential" content, not Fregean sense. (A notable exception is the theory discussed in Section 4.5.)

With this general picture of naturalistic theories of content in hand, let us now look at some prominent proposals.

4.1 Causal Theories

Mental representations are often caused by the things they represent: perceptual representations of spherical objects are caused by spherical objects, the belief that a certain person is present is caused by the presence of that particular person, the belief that it is raining is caused by the fact that it is raining and so on. In light of this commonplace observation, it is natural to conjecture that causation may well play a key role in the explanation of representational

---

[25] In fact, almost all of the accounts discussed in the following are restricted to the class of descriptive representations or to some subclass thereof. For accounts that aim to explain various types of representations that are not (or not purely) descriptive, see Martínez (2011), Pavese (2017), Cochrane (2018), Bergman (2019) and Schulte (2019b).

[26] The idea of "directions of fit" goes back to Anscombe (1957, 56) and is developed further in Platts (1979, 256–275).

content. If we develop this conjecture into a theory, we get a *causal theory of content*.

In order to highlight the challenges faced by causal theories of content (and naturalistic theories in general), it is useful to start with an exceedingly simple theory. I will call it the *crude causal theory* (*CCT*) (taking my cue from Fodor 1987, 99). This theory identifies the content of a representation with the state or event that always causes this representation – with its "constant cause," as we might say. More precisely, the theory says that, for any internal state type R of some physical system:

(CCT) R is a descriptive representation with the content p iff (and because) tokens of R are always caused by tokens of the state that p.[27]

To illustrate, according to CCT, my neural state N represents that a cow is present iff tokens of type N are always caused by the presence of a cow.

Before we come to the evaluation of this theory, let me briefly note two things. First, CCT is not completely general but restricted to descriptive ("belief-like") representations. Secondly, for this restricted class of representations, CCT answers both the status and the content question: it says that an internal state of a physical system is a representation iff it has a constant cause and identifies its content with that constant cause.

On reflection, it is obvious that CCT is untenable. There are many problems with it, but I will only mention three of the most fundamental, since these are the problems that will resurface again in discussions of other, more sophisticated theories.

The Problem of Error and The "Disjunction Problem"

First, CCT does not allow for misrepresentation. Since the state R can only have the content *a cow is present* if every single token of R is caused by a cow, R must be true whenever it is tokened. Hence, CCT fails to capture one of the most central features of representational states. This is known as the problem of error.

Essentially the same difficulty can also be brought out in a different way. Suppose that my neural state N is, in fact, the state that we would ordinarily describe as my belief that a cow is present: N disposes me to assent to statements

---

[27] A brief comment on the expression "iff (and because)." The "because" has been added to make it explicit that the theory aims to provide an *explanation* of content, with the explanandum on the left-hand side and the explanans on the right-hand side. The reason for the "iff"/"if and only if" has two parts: first, since the explanation is constitutive, the explanans is commonly supposed to be *metaphysically sufficient* for the explanandum (hence the "if"); secondly, since the explanation applies to *all* descriptive representations, the explanans must also be at least *materially necessary* for the explanandum (hence the "only if"). For the sake of simplicity, I will drop the "(and because)" in the following.

like "there's a cow," causes many other kinds of cow-appropriate behavior and is often caused by cows. However, N is also sometimes caused by other things, for example by cow replicas, cow holograms, cow-like horses at dawn and by "moo" sounds coming from carefully hidden stereo speakers. According to CCT, if N has any content at all, it cannot be the content that a cow is present (as folk psychology would have it). Instead, N's content must be *that a cow or a cow replica or a cow hologram or . . . is present*, since the only state that can be described as a constant cause of N is the disjunctive state that a cow or a cow replica or a cow hologram or . . . is present. Hence, CCT ascribes wildly disjunctive contents to ordinary belief states and that is clearly unacceptable. This difficulty, which can be seen as the flip side of the problem of error, is called "the disjunction problem" (cf. Fodor 1984/1990, 1990a).[28]

The Problem of Content Indeterminacy

Another major problem – and one that is clearly distinct from the problem of error – is the problem of content indeterminacy. Let us assume, for the sake of the argument, that my N-states are, in fact, always caused by the presence of a cow. In this case, CCT entails that N has the content *a cow is present*. The problem is that CCT seems to entail that N has many other contents as well. This content indeterminacy or "content multiplicity" (Bergman 2023, 307) arises in two ways, yielding two distinct subproblems. First, note that all cows are also animals, as well as biological organisms. Hence, in our hypothetical scenario it is not only true that (i) N-states are always caused by the presence of a cow but also (ii) that they are always caused by the presence of an animal and (iii) that they are always caused by the presence of a biological organism. So, it seems that, according to CCT, N has the contents *an animal is present* and *a biological organism is present* in addition to the content *a cow is present*. This version of the indeterminacy problem is (what I will call) the *characterization problem*.[29]

Secondly, it is obvious that all N-state tokens in our scenario stand at the end of long *chains* of causes. Such a chain will always include (i) a certain kind of nerve signal, (ii) a certain pattern of sensory stimulation, (iii) a bundle of light waves/sound waves/ . . . of a certain kind traveling through space and (iv) the presence of a cow (as well as other, more distal causes, which we will ignore for the present). Of course, the intermediate causes (i)–(iii) will be very different for different tokens of N, but it seems that we can construct a *disjunctive* state at

---

[28] The term "disjunction problem" is sometimes also used in a wider sense, so I will generally speak of the "problem of error" instead.

[29] This problem is also known as the "vertical problem" (Prinz 2000, 12; after Godfrey-Smith 1989) or the "breadth ambiguity" (Sterelny 1990, 113).

each of these levels that will qualify as a constant cause of N. Hence, prima facie, CCT also ascribes (disjunctive) contents concerning nerve signals, sensory stimulation and other intermediate causes to N. This second version of the problem of indeterminacy is known in the literature as the *distality problem*.[30]

The Problem of Pansemanticism

A third fundamental problem concerns CCT's answer to the status question. According to CCT, *every* internal state of a physical object that has a constant cause is a (descriptive) representation. If constant causes can be highly disjunctive (as we have just assumed), almost every physical object has internal states that qualify as representational. Surprisingly, it turns out that representational systems are literally everywhere. This problem is sometimes dubbed the problem of "pansemanticism" (Fodor 1990b, 92) or the "breadth-of-application problem" (Burge 2010, 205).

No one has ever seriously held CCT. But there are views in its vicinity that have been defended in the literature. Some of these views take the following form: they distinguish between two types of situations, "type one situations" and "type two situations," and identify the content of a representational state with its constant cause *in type one situations*.[31] Such theories are sometimes called "type one theories." Here is, in a bit more detail, a sketch for a (comparatively) modest type one theory (*MTT*) that is restricted to descriptive representations and only addresses the content question for these representations:

(MTT) If R is a descriptive representation, then R has the content p iff, *in situations of type F*, tokens of R are always caused by tokens of the state that p.

A clear advantage of this type of theory over CTT is that it can avoid the problem of error, as long as it is possible for tokens of R to occur in situations that are not of type F. But, of course, the crucial task for proponents of MTT is to specify what these "situations of type F" (i.e., the type one situations) actually are. It is easy to see that they cannot simply be specified as "situations that ensure the truth of R." Such a characterization would not only be inconsistent with the naturalistic goal of explaining representational content in non-semantic terms; it would also completely trivialize the account. Neither can situations of type F be defined as "epistemically optimal situations," for similar reasons. A more promising approach would be to characterize type F situations as

---

[30] It is also called the "horizontal problem" (Prinz 2000, 12; after Godfrey-Smith 1989) or the "depth ambiguity" (Sterelny 1990, 113).

[31] This general characterization is due to Fodor (1990a, 60).

"biologically normal situations," or as "situations which guarantee the well-functioning of the R-producing mechanisms." This is (roughly) the account sketched by Dennis Stampe (1977), but since it involves an appeal to biological functions, it belongs to the class of teleological theories of content, which will be discussed in Section 4.4.

A very different kind of causal theory has been developed by Jerry Fodor (1987, 1990b). It is called the *asymmetric dependence theory* (*ADT*), and it treats the contents of *concepts* as primary explananda. (In this context, the term "concept" is to be understood in the "mental particulars sense"; following Fodor, we can think of concepts in this sense as words in a language of thought; see Section 2.2.) Very roughly, the basic idea of ADT is this: the tokens of any concept C have many different kinds of causes, but there is always one kind K of causes that is special. Namely, it is special in the sense that the causal-nomological relationships between all *other* kinds of causes K*, K**, ... and C (i.e., the *ceteris paribus* laws that link causes of kinds K*, K**, ... to C) depend on the causal-nomological relationship between causes of kind K and C (i.e., on the *ceteris paribus* law that links causes of kind K to C), but not vice versa. In other words, causes of kind K are special because the relationships between all other kinds of causes and C are *asymmetrically dependent* on the K–C relationship.

To understand this rather abstract characterization, it is helpful to consider a simple example. Suppose that COW is a word of my language of thought (my "Mentalese") and that COW tokens are often caused by cows but also (on rare occasions) by cats. Still, according to Fodor, COW means *cow* instead of *cat* or *cow or cat* as long as "there being cat-caused COW tokens depends on there being cow-caused COW tokens, but not the other way around" (Fodor 1990b: 91; with "COW" substituted for "'cow'," for the sake of consistency).[32] This asymmetric dependence relationship can also be spelled out in terms of coun-terfactuals: if cows didn't cause COW tokens, cats would not cause COW tokens either; but if cats didn't cause COW tokens, cows would *still* cause COW tokens (Fodor 1987, 108).

As Fodor points out, these considerations are sufficient to show that the asymmetric dependence theory can account for the possibility of misrepresen-tation. If COW can mean *cow* even though COW tokens are sometimes caused by cats, then a (token) belief that involves the Mentalese sentence THERE'S A COW can mean *there's a cow* while being caused by a cat, and thus be false. Fodor also argues at length that his theory can avoid several other

---

[32] Of course, COW only has *cow* as its determinate meaning if what is true for cats also holds, *mutatis mutandis*, for all other alternative causes of COW.

problems, for example the problem of indeterminacy and the problem of pansemanticism, and that it is not subject to counterexamples proposed by Baker (1991), Boghossian (1991) and other critics (Fodor 1990b, 1991).

However, many opponents of Fodor would argue that there is a fundamental difficulty with his proposal: it is utterly mysterious, even in mundane cases, why we should think that the required asymmetric dependence relationships actually hold.[33] Let us look again at my COW concept and the associated counterfactuals that are supposed to establish that COW means *cow* instead of *cat*: (i) if cows didn't cause COW tokens, cats would not cause COW tokens either and (ii) if cats didn't cause COW tokens, cows would still cause COW tokens. Are these counterfactuals true? For the sake of brevity, let us grant the truth of (ii) and focus on (i). Roughly speaking, (i) is true if the closest possible worlds where cows do not cause COW tokens (the closest "no-cow-COW worlds") are also worlds where cats do not cause COW tokens ("no-cat-COW worlds"). Now, we might think that the closest no-cow-COW worlds are simply worlds where I have never encountered cows, or never attended to them, so that I never developed a COW concept linked to certain types of sensory input (visual perceptions of cow-like shapes, auditory perceptions of "moo" sounds, etc.). It is very plausible that such worlds are also no-cat-COW worlds, that is, worlds where cats do not cause COW tokens either. Hence, counterfactual (i) would come out as true.

However, Fodor insists that this is *not* the right interpretation of the counterfactuals (for good reasons, since this interpretation allows for the construction of quite convincing counterexamples; cf. Fodor 1987, 109; Adams 2021, sec. 3.4). The counterfactuals are not to be read "diachronically," as referring to possible worlds where cows do not cause COW tokens now because the past in these worlds has been different, but "synchronically," as referring to possible worlds where the causal-nomological relationship between cows and COW tokens breaks down *at the present moment* (Fodor 1987, 109; 1991, 292). Strikingly, though, Fodor never gives any detailed account of what, in his view, happens in these possible worlds and why we are justified in maintaining that *all* causal-nomological relationships between non-cows and COW tokens also break down in these worlds. (If, for instance, the relevant no-cow-COW worlds were the closest possible worlds where all cows vanish into thin air at this very moment, it seems clear that some non-cows would continue to cause COW tokens!) Hence, it remains fundamentally unclear how Fodor's account is supposed to work, even in the paradigmatic cases. This is presumably one of the

---

[33] Different versions of this worry have been articulated, for example, by Millikan (1991, 153–154), Rupert (2008, 360–361) and Loewer (2017, 184).

main reasons why the asymmetric dependence theory has not won many converts to date.[34]

There are several other interesting causal theories that have been defended in the literature, but most of them combine the causal story with other elements – for example, with an appeal to biological functions or to probabilistic relationships. Some of these "hybrid" accounts will be discussed in the next two sections.

4.2 Informational Theories

Another attractive starting point for theories of mental content is the notion of *information*. Scientists standardly describe perceptual and cognitive processes as types of "information processing" going on in the brain and say that the neural states involved in these processes "carry information about" things or events in the outside world. This suggests that informational relationships may be crucial for the explanation of representational content.

The earliest and most influential informational theory of content is the account developed by Fred Dretske in his book *Knowledge and the Flow of Information* (1981). Dretske starts with a detailed analysis of the notion of information. According to Dretske, this notion is supposed to capture the relationship that holds, for example, between smoke and fire, tree rings and tree age or quail tracks and quail: the fact that there is smoke over there carries the information that there is a fire over there; the fact that this tree has thirty-two rings carries the information that it is thirty-two years old; and the fact that there are quail tracks on the ground carries the information that quail were here recently.[35]

In order to define information, Dretske appeals to the notion of conditional probability: what it means for the state of smoke being over there to carry the information that fire is over there is, roughly speaking, that the conditional probability of fire being over there, given that smoke is over there, equals 1, i.e., that P(fire over there|smoke over there) = 1 (Dretske 1981, 65).[36] In other words, the presence of smoke must guarantee the presence of fire in order to carry information about it. One qualification that Dretske adds is that it is only

---

[34] For more detailed criticisms of the theory, see Adams and Aizawa (1994), Mendola (2003) and Greenberg (2006).

[35] States that carry the information that p have also been described as "indicating" that p, as being "natural signs" of p, and as having the "natural meaning" that p.

[36] In addition to that, Dretske requires that the prior probability of fire being over there must be less than 1, that is, that P(fire over there) < 1. Furthermore, information is relativized to the state of knowledge of a subject (Dretske 1981, 78), but since it is clear that this part of the definition must be removed if the notion of information is to be appealed to in a naturalistic explanation of representational content, we can ignore it here.

under certain "channel conditions" that this strong connection between the state types *smoke (at location l and time t)* and *fire (at location l and time t)* needs to hold and that it is only under those conditions that tokens of the first state carry the information that the second state obtains.[37]

Given this definition of information, it follows that there is no such thing as "misinformation" (Dretske 1981, 45). To be sure, there can be situations where there is smoke without fire but, by definition, these must be situations where the channel conditions do not hold, so that these tokens of smoke (at l and t) do *not* carry the information that there is fire (at l and t).

This already makes it clear that a state's representational content cannot be *identified* with its informational content (i.e., with the information that it carries). Like the simplistic causal theory CCT (discussed in Section 4.1), a theory that simply equates representational and informational content would be unable to explain misrepresentation and would presumably have all (or most) of the other problems of CCT as well. Thus it is no surprise that Dretske (1981) does not adopt such a theory. Instead, he proposes a more complex informational account: focusing on "beliefs of the form 'This is F' where *this* is the perceptual object [. . .] and *F* is an expression of some ostensively learned simple concept" (Dretske 1981, 212), he suggests that the representational content of such a belief is fixed by a certain type of information that its tokens carry toward the end of the "learning period", that is, the period of acquiring the concept *F* (Dretske 1981, 193–195). On this account, it is possible that beliefs with the representational content *p* that occur *after* the end of the learning period do not carry the information that p, and these beliefs can be false. Dretske thus succeeds in solving the problem of error. However, his account still faces a number of other problems, many of which pertain to the notion of a learning period and the assumptions Dretske makes concerning it (Fodor 1990a; Loewer 2017). Problems of this kind were probably the reason why Dretske himself gave up his purely informational theory in favor a of a teleological-informational approach (see Section 4.4).

However, there is another fundamental difficulty for Dretske's account and that is his strict definition of the notion of information, combined with his appeal to "channel conditions." If the channel conditions that enable the state F to carry the information that the state G obtains are required to be such that the F-state must *guarantee* that the G-state obtains, then these conditions cannot merely be the stable background conditions (concerning gravity, atmospheric pressure, the presence of oxygen, etc.) that we ordinarily rely on in formulating causal

---

[37] Roughly speaking, Dretske's channel conditions are something like stable background conditions (Dretske 1981, 115, 119), but giving a precise definition of them generates considerable problems, as we will see later in this section.

generalizations. Clearly, such background conditions would not yield conditional probabilities of 1. So what else is included in Dretske's channel conditions? Unfortunately, no clear answer to this question is to be found in Dretske's writings. Sometimes, he appears to suggest that channel conditions are relative to the beliefs or attitudes of the observer (Dretske 1981, 115; 1983, 84), but that would (arguably) undermine the naturalistic credentials of his informational theory of content, since it would make the notion of information implicitly mentalistic (Loewer 1983). Moreover, it would mean that Dretske can no longer claim to offer a realist theory of representation that treats content properties as objective, observer-independent features of cognitive systems (Sosa 1983). So, this crucial question is left wide open.

For this reason (among others), contemporary proponents of informational theories of content generally reject Dretske's strict definition of information. In line with the mathematical theory of information pioneered by Claude Shannon (1948), they accept that information can be grounded in weaker probabilistic relationships than conditional probabilities of 1. Some theorists maintain, for instance, that a state F carries the information that another state G obtains if the conditional probability of G being tokened given that F is tokened is greater than the prior probability of G, that is, if F's being tokened "raises" the probability of G's being tokened (see Lloyd 1989, 64; Price 2001, 92, 98; cf. also Shea 2018, 76). According to this definition, a column of smoke over there carries the information that fire is over there because it raises the probability of fire being over there.[38]

Moreover, contemporary proponents of informational theories usually combine information-theoretic requirements for content with other conditions. Some theorists add a teleological element to their account; others propose an additional causal requirement.[39] Since theories of the first type are discussed in Section 4.4, my focus here will be on purely causal-informational theories, which include the accounts developed by Dan Lloyd (1989), Robert Rupert (1999, 2008), Chris Eliasmith (2005, 2013) and Marius Usher (2001).

All of these accounts are quite complex, and some of them raise considerable questions of interpretation. To avoid getting lost in the details, I will restrict my attention to a theory that can with some justification be attributed to Usher, but

---

[38] For more on the recent debate about information, see, for example, Scarantino (2015), Fresco et al. (2020) and Fresco (2021).

[39] An exception is Manolo Martínez (2019), who offers a purely informational account of representation "for a certain important family of cases" (Martínez 2019, 1214). However, even Martínez holds that "teleofunctions have a role to play in a complete theory of representation" (Martínez 2019, 1215).

which also resembles the proposals of Eliasmith and Rupert in certain respects. I will call it *Usher's informational theory* (*UIT*) (cf. Usher 2001, 320–323):

(UIT) If C is a concept (of subject S), then C has the content F iff

i. the presence of an F can cause C,

ii. P(C is tokened|an F is present) > P(C is tokened|an F* is present) for all F* distinct from F which can cause C, and

iii. P(an F is present|C is tokened) > P(an F is present|C* is tokened) for all concepts C* (of S) distinct from C.

According to this theory, my concept COW means *cow* (instead of *cat* or *cat or cow*) if the following three conditions are fulfilled. First, cows cause tokens of COW. Secondly, among the many causes of COW tokens, cows are the most "efficient": they are more likely to cause COW tokens than cats or cats-or-cows are. (In other words, a cow is the "best predictor" of a COW token among the causes of COW.) Thirdly, it is more likely that a cow is present given that COW is tokened than given that any of my other concepts (CAT, DOG, ANIMAL, etc.) is tokened. (A COW token is the "best predictor" of a cow among my concepts.)

It is obvious that Usher's theory solves the problem of error (since it allows for COW tokens that mean cow but are sometimes caused by non-cows). However, much like Dretske's proposal, UIT faces several other serious difficulties. I will briefly discuss two of them.[40]

First, UIT seems to fall prey to a version of the distality problem: the contents it assigns to concepts are often *too proximal* (Artiga and Sebastián 2020, 620–622; Roche and Sober 2021). Consider an ordinary situation where I see a cow very clearly and distinctly and come to form the belief THERE'S A COW. In this situation, the COW token is caused not only by the cow but also by the specific retinal image that the cow projects onto the retina (an image of type T). Very plausibly, this type of retinal image is more likely to cause COW tokens than cows are. Furthermore, although COW is often tokened without an image of type T being present, it is plausible that a T-image being present is more likely given that COW tokened than given a tokening of any other of my concepts. Hence, UIT entails that COW means *retinal image of type T* instead of *cow*. Interestingly, this is not just an unfortunate feature of this particular informational theory: Roche and Sober (2021) have shown for a wide range of causal-informational theories (which they call "purely probabilistic causal theories") that none of them can

---

[40] For further objections, see Artiga and Sebastián (2020).

solve both the distality problem *and* the problem of error (or disjunction problem).

Secondly, the theory seems to be incomplete in an important respect. Note that we can ask, concerning the conditional probabilities in clauses (ii) and (iii), *under what conditions* the probabilities are supposed to hold.[41] It is implausible to claim that they are supposed to hold under "conditions-in-the-universe-any-place-any-time" (Millikan 1989, 281) – for one thing because this would make it hard or even impossible to estimate these probabilities but also because it would lead to wrong results in many cases (e.g., when a particular C changes its content over time). An alternative would be to say that the probabilities are supposed to hold under *biologically normal conditions*, but that would introduce a teleological element into the theory, which runs contrary to the intentions of Usher and the other proponents of purely causal-informational theories of content. Hence, UIT leaves a crucial question unanswered.

4.3 Structuralist Theories

Like causal and informational theories of content, structuralist theories are inspired by a very simple idea. In this case, it is the idea that representational content derives, at least in part, from a relation of *similarity*. This idea seems natural when we look at the way in which statues or pictures represent. Prima facie, a bust of Lon Chaney represents Lon Chaney's head because it *resembles* his head in certain respects, and the same apparently holds for a picture of Hollywood Boulevard that represents a particular section of this famous Hollywood street.

However, when we apply this idea to mental representations, it seems like a nonstarter. The Lon Chaney bust resembles Lon Chaney's head because it has (roughly) the *same shape* as Lon Chaney's head. But how could a *mental* representation of Lon Chaney's head or any other material object ever have the same shape as that object or have any other characteristic properties (like size or color) in common with it? From a dualist perspective, this seems impossible (because, presumably, nonmaterial entities do not possess the properties in question), and from a naturalist perspective, it seems at least exceedingly unlikely (because, as far as we know, our brains do not contain little replicas of the things we are looking at or thinking about).

This is where the important distinction between first-order and second-order similarity comes in. A relation of *first-order similarity* obtains between two entities, x and y, if x and y share one or more properties, for example if they have

---

[41] This is a version of the "reference class problem" discussed by Millikan (1989, 281; 2004, 37–40) and Shea (2018, 79–80).

the same size, shape, color or mass. A relation of *second-order similarity*, by contrast, obtains between two sets, A and B, when certain relations between the objects in set A are "mirrored" by relations between the objects in set B.[42] For instance, there is a relation of second-order similarity between the set {1, 2, 3} and the set {John Barrymore, John Drew Barrymore, Drew Barrymore}, because the relation of *being smaller than* on the first set is "mirrored" by the relation of *being the father of* on the second if we map 1 to John Barrymore, 2 to John Drew Barrymore and 3 to Drew Barrymore.

This distinction suggests that similarity might play a role in the explanation of content after all – not first-order similarity, which is almost certainly irrelevant for mental content, but second-order similarity. And this is, indeed, the basic idea of "similarity-based" or "structuralist" accounts of content, which is worked out in different ways by Chris Swoyer (1991), Robert Cummins (1996), Paul Churchland (2001/2007, 2012), Randy Gallistel and Adam Philip King (2010) and others.[43]

One structuralist account that is currently very influential is the theory proposed by Gerard O'Brien and Jon Opie (2004; see also O'Brien 2015). The notion that is central to the theory of O'Brien and Opie (henceforth O&O) is the notion of "structural resemblance," a type of second-order similarity that is "based on the *physical* relations among a set of representing vehicles" (O'Brien and Opie 2004, 14). They define this notion in the following way: "one system *structurally resembles* another when the physical relations among the objects that comprise the first preserve some aspects of the relational organization of the objects that comprise the second" (O'Brien and Opie 2004, 15).

The term "physical relations" is used by O&O in a somewhat peculiar sense that excludes causal relations but seems to include virtually all other natural relationships, like spatial relations, differences in physical magnitudes and so on (O'Brien and Opie 2004, 15).[44] By defining structural resemblance as a relation that is grounded in "physical" relations between representing vehicles, they aim to differentiate their view from causal role theories of content (see Section 4.5).

As O&O point out, maps and diagrams are good examples of external representations that stand in structural resemblance relations to the things they

---

[42] This is only a rough characterization, of course. For a precise definition of second-order similarity, see O'Brien and Opie (2004, 11).

[43] It should be noted that these theories are distant descendants of the "picture theory" of meaning (Wittgenstein 1921/2003).

[44] Importantly, the restriction to "physical relations" (as O&O use the term) also excludes relations in the purely mathematical sense, which can be understood as (arbitrary) sets of ordered pairs. Since relations in this sense are extremely "cheap," they must be excluded in order to avoid trivializing the structural resemblance requirement (see Shea 2013).

represent. An ordinary map of Italy, for instance, contains points (marked "Milan," "Rome," "Naples," etc.) that stand in spatial relations to each other which preserve the spatial relations between Italian cities (Milan, Rome, Naples, etc.). More interestingly, a bar chart showing average daily temperature for different months contains bars that differ from each other in height (bar #1 is higher than bar #2 and lower than bar #3, etc.), and these differences in height preserve differences in temperature (January was hotter than February and colder than March, etc.). Crucially, O&O argue that we have reason to believe that such structural resemblance relations also obtain between neuronal vehicles and the things they represent, thus enabling an explanation of mental representation/content in terms of structural resemblance (O'Brien and Opie 2004, 15–17).

However, structural resemblance alone would leave content highly indeterminate. A set of neural states that stands in a structural resemblance relation to one set of states/objects will presumably stand in that relation to countless other sets of states/objects as well, if no further restrictions are in place. This is a difficulty that O&O are aware of, and they have a reply ready. According to their view, it is a constitutive feature of representations that they are "interpreted" in some way. In the case of mental representations, "interpretation" can be equated with the "modification of a cognitive subject's *behavioural dispositions*" (O'Brien and Opie 2004, 5). Hence, they can say that the content-grounding relation is "a relation of structural resemblance between mental representing vehicles and their objects *that disposes cognitive subjects to behave appropriately towards the latter*" (O'Brien and Opie 2004, 15; my emphasis). Or, as O'Brien puts it in a later paper: first, "a system's behavioural dispositions … anchor its representing vehicles to particular represented domains," and then, structural resemblance relations "determine the content of the individual vehicles" (O'Brien 2015, 11).

According to O&O, the structuralist theory of content has a major advantage over rival accounts, since it is the only naturalistic theory that can adequately account for the causal relevance of content properties (O'Brien and Opie 2004, 3). To understand this point, we must briefly consider a well-known problem for standard naturalistic theories of content, sometimes called "the problem of content epiphenomenalism" or "the Soprano problem" (after Dretske 1988, 80). This problem runs as follows. Causal and informational theories entail that, for any individual J, the content properties of J's brain states are not determined by how J's brain is like intrinsically but by the causal or informational relations in which these brain states stand to external states of affairs. (The same holds, *mutatis mutandis*, for teleological theories of content, as we will see in Section 4.4.) However, the causal role that these brain states play in bringing about J's behavior seems to depend only on the intrinsic nature of J's brain. Hence, causal and informational (and teleological) theories appear to make content *causally irrelevant* for behavior: if Groucho's belief that there is money in the safe causes him to crack the safe, then it does *not* do so in virtue of being a belief that there is money in the safe but in virtue of being a neurophysiological state of a certain type (etc.). This seems to be a highly implausible consequence.

According to O&O, their theory avoids the problem of content epiphenomenalism. They point to the fact that, on their view, the content properties of J's neuronal vehicles are grounded in "physical" relations between them, which are intrinsic to J's brain, and can thus play a genuine causal role in the production of J's behavior (O'Brien and Opie 2004, 18).

An immediate worry about this line of argument is that, on a natural interpretation of O&O's theory, content is not exclusively grounded in the "physical" relations between neuronal vehicles; it is *also* partly grounded in J's behavioral dispositions and in how they relate to J's environment. If this is correct, then content properties are partly constituted by external factors, and the problem of content epiphenomenalism remains.[45] Hence, the supposed advantage of the theory disappears. (A more elaborate structuralist account of the explanatory relevance of content properties is offered by Gladziejewski and Milkowski 2017, who draw on an interventionist analysis of causation; for criticism, see Nirshberg and Shapiro 2021, 7652–7653.)

Another advantage that is often claimed for structuralist theories of content/ representation is that they are more restrictive than (some) of their rivals. While standard causal and informational theories seem to be committed to the claim that mere "indicator states" are contentful, structuralist theories can supposedly avoid this consequence (Ramsey 2007; Gladziejewski and Milkowski 2017). A common example for "indicator states" are the internal states that control the behavior of a thermostat. Suppose that the thermostat contains a bimetallic strip whose curvature varies with the room temperature. When the strip's curvature is less than 25° (at a temperature of less than 18°C), it makes contact with a pin, thereby switching on the heating unit. Arguably, it is implausible to categorize the state of the strip's curvature being less than 25° as a representation with the content *the room temperature is less than 18°C*.[46] Structuralists claim that they can avoid this consequence. They point out that the internal state in question – the strip's curvature being less than 25° – is very much unlike a map: it does not contain several different constituents that stand in relations to each other which

---

[45] For a related worry, see Nirshberg and Shapiro (2021, 7651–7652).

[46] For a discussion of the assumption that indicator states should not be categorized as representations, see Section 8.2.

preserve relations between different objects in the environment. In other words, there is in this case no set of inner items that could stand in a structural resemblance relationship to a set of external objects, and thus the state of the bimetallic strip does not qualify as a genuine representation.

However, as several authors have pointed out, we do in fact find a structural resemblance relation if we consider the set of *different* strip curvatures (say, from 0° to 25°) and the set of corresponding room temperatures (Morgan 2014; Nirshberg and Shapiro 2021). In this case, the differences in degree of curvature preserve the differences in degree of temperature, so the definition of structural resemblance is satisfied. And the same strategy seems to work even for simple on-off devices. Again, the advantage for structuralism appears to vanish under close inspection.[47]

Still, the structuralist approach is clearly of great interest for semantic naturalists and well worth exploring further – either in its pure form or in the form of a "hybrid" approach that combines structuralist ideas with other elements (see, e.g., Shea 2018).

4.4 Teleological Theories

The teleological approach, or teleosemantics, is currently the dominant naturalistic approach to the explanation of mental content, and thus a great variety of teleological theories are to be found in the literature. What unifies these theories is one defining characteristic: they all appeal, at some point in their explanation, to a teleological notion of function (i.e., to a notion of function that allows for the possibility of malfunction). In a bit more detail, the core idea of teleosemantics is this: in order to explain how states can have content, we need to explain how they can be accurate or inaccurate, true or false, realized or unrealized (see Section 2.2), and in order to do that, we need to appeal (in some way or other) to the distinction between proper functioning and malfunctioning.

To get a better grip on this approach, let us start with the notion of function. Typically, teleosemanticists subscribe to an *etiological* account of functions (although there are exceptions; cf. Nanay 2014; Bauer 2017; Piccinini 2020).[48] In its simplest form, an etiological account says that (biological) functions are always directly grounded in natural selection processes: a trait has the function to φ iff it was selected for φ-ing by a process of natural selection. If we try to

---

[47] For a response to this argument, see Gladziejewski and Milkowski (2017, 347–352); for further discussion of the advantages and disadvantages of structuralism, see Lee (2019) and Facchin (2021b).

[48] For a critical discussion of these non-etiological or "ahistorical" versions of teleosemantics, see Hundertmark (2018).

express this idea with greater precision, we get something like the following *simple etiological account* (*SEA*):

(SEA) A token t of type T has the function to φ iff (i) earlier tokens of T have φ-ed, and (ii) the fact that earlier tokens of T have φ-ed helps to explain why T was selected for in a process of natural selection.[49]

According to SEA, the stripes of a present-day zebra have the function to deter parasitic insects because (i) earlier tokens of the type *zebra stripes* have deterred parasitic insects and (ii) the fact that earlier tokens of the type *zebra stripes* have deterred parasitic insects helps to explain why zebra stripes were selected for, that is, why the striped pattern was favored by natural selection over rival patterns, thus becoming dominant in the zebra's ancestor populations and remaining dominant from then on.

There are different ways of modifying SEA, and it is usually one of these modified etiological accounts that proponents of teleological theories accept. Here, I will only mention the most important modification: teleosemanticists generally insist that not all functions are directly grounded in processes of natural selection. Some maintain that functions can also be grounded in other selection processes (like operant conditioning, neural selection or cultural selection),[50] some hold that they can be *indirectly* grounded in processes of natural selection (cf. Millikan's notion of "derived" proper functions developed in Millikan 1984, chap. 2), and there are also further options.[51]

In surveys of teleological accounts of content, it is customary to distinguish between two types of theories: (i) theories that focus more on the *input-side* of cognitive processes and on the mechanisms that produce representational states (the "producers") and (ii) theories that emphasize the *output-side* and the mechanisms that respond to representational states by (ultimately) generating behavior (the "consumers"). The input-oriented theories include Stampe's (1977) account, which identifies the content of a descriptive representation with its constant cause under normal conditions (see Section 4.1), as well as Dretske's (1986, 1988) later teleological-informational theory, which says (in a nutshell) that a state R is a descriptive representation with the content p iff R has the function of carrying the information that p.[52] A more recent input-oriented theory, and arguably the

---

[49] Definitions similar to SEA have been offered by Neander (1991, 173–174) and Godfrey-Smith (1994, 359). Another closely related proposal is Millikan's (1984, chap. 1). For a more recent etiological account, see Garson's (2017, 2019a) "generalized selected effects theory."

[50] On these issues, see especially Garson (2019a, 65–92).

[51] See, for example, Shea (2018, 57–59), who proposes that functions can also be grounded in processes of self-maintenance or persistence.

[52] Further input-oriented theories have been proposed by Matthen (1988) and Jacob (1997).

most sophisticated of its kind, is Karen Neander's (2013, 2017) "informational teleosemantics," which I will now discuss in more detail.

First, it is important to note that Neander's informational teleosemantics (IT) is restricted to perceptual representations and that it only aims to answer the content question for these representations, while remaining silent on the status question. The theory's core idea is that the content of a perceptual representation is determined by a certain function, the so-called response function, of its producer. Here is a preliminary way of spelling out this idea (cf. Neander 2013, 30; 2017, 151):

(IT) If R is a perceptual state, then R has the content p iff R's producer has the function of producing R (specifically) in response to the state that p.[53]

To see how IT works, consider an example that is discussed in great detail by Neander herself: the case of the prey-catching toad. Simplifying a bit, the prey-catching behavior of the common toad can be described in the following way: when (and only when) a small, dark, moving object appears in the toad's visual field, its visual system generates a certain kind of brain state (namely, activation of T5-2 neurons, or "T5-2+," for short), which then causes snapping behavior.[54] Since most small, dark, moving objects in the toad's natural habitat are prey animals, this type of behavior is evolutionary beneficial.

Neander assumes that T5-2+ states count as perceptual representations and argues, on this basis, that IT ascribes the content *a small, dark, moving object is present* to T5-2+ states, because the toad's visual system (the "producer") has the function of producing these states in response to the presence of small, dark, moving objects (Neander 2017, 159). But how, one might ask, can Neander claim that the visual system has this particular response function, rather than (say) the function of producing T5-2+ states in response to *prey animals* or to *nutritious objects*? This is an important question indeed, since a failure to answer it would give rise to a version of the indeterminacy problem (namely, to the characterization problem; see Section 4.1). Fortunately, Neander does provide an answer to this question (Neander 2017, chap. 7). First, she points out that she understands the term "responding" in a strong causal sense: a mechanism can only have the function of responding to the presence of an F by producing an R if the property of being F is *causally relevant* for bringing it about that the mechanism produces an R. But in the case of the toad, neither the object's being a prey animal (i.e., a member of one of the toad's prey species)

---

[53] I have added the word "specifically" to indicate that the producer fails to perform its function not only if it does not produce R in response to a token of the state that p but also if it *does* respond with the production of R to something that is *not* a token of the state that p.

[54] For a more accurate and detailed description of the process, see Neander (2017, chap. 5).

nor its being nutritious is causally relevant for bringing it about that the visual system produces a T5-2+ state, only the object's being small, dark and moving is (as can easily be tested by varying these properties independently). Hence, the system only has the function of responding to a small, dark, moving object, and the specter of indeterminacy is averted.

Neander also restates IT by using the concept of information (see, e.g., Neander 2013, 30). This is possible because she defines information in purely causal terms (Neander 2017, 142–145); but since this conception of information is not an essential ingredient of her account, I will omit it here.

We have seen that Neander's preliminary account, IT, seems to be able to solve the characterization problem, and it is obvious that it can also account for the possibility of error (since cases where the producer does not fulfill its response function are perfectly possible). Nevertheless, there are some weighty objections that can be raised against IT.

Some critics object to the notion of a response function (Millikan 2013; see Neander 2017, 132–133 for a reply). Others focus on the fact that IT entails that properties can only be represented in perception if they are causally relevant for the production of perceptual representations. They argue that this "causal requirement" yields implausible content ascriptions (Green 2017; Ganson 2021). Finally, Neander herself suggests that IT is unable to solve the distality problem (Neander 2013, 33; 2017, 217–221). Consider the causal chain that leads from (a) the small, dark, moving object through (b) a pattern of light and (c) a pattern of retinal stimulation to the state of T5-2 activation. According to Neander, the toad's visual system has, *for each of the states (a)–(c)*, the function to produce T5-2 activation in response to that state (call them "function$_a$," "function$_b$" and "function$_c$"). Of course, these functions are closely related: the visual system performs function$_a$ *by* performing function$_b$, and function$_b$ *by* performing function$_c$. Still, all of the three functions are genuine response functions, so IT entails that the content of T5-2+ is indeterminate between *a small, dark, moving object is present*, *a pattern of light of type L is present* and *a retinal stimulation pattern of type S is present*. Neander tries to solve this problem by adding a "distality principle" to IT,[55] but it is controversial whether her solution is successful (for discussion, see Schulte 2018, 2022; Garson 2019b).[56]

---

[55] The distality principle says, in effect, that the response function that is performed by performing all the other response functions (if any) determines the content of the perceptual representation (Neander 2017, 222). Note that Neander also modifies IT in another way, by adding a condition of second-order similarity (Neander 2017, chap. 8).

[56] Further interesting problems for Neander's proposal have been raised by Hundertmark (2021), Egan (2022) and Hill (2022). For replies to Egan and Hill on behalf of Neander, see Garson (2022).

Let us move on to the second group of theories, which are often described as "output-oriented" or "consumer" theories. What they all have in common is that they put a strong emphasis on how mental representations are *used* within a system. One such theory, for which the label "output-oriented" is clearly apt, is David Papineau's "desire-first view" (Papineau 1984, 1993, 1998). According to Papineau, the content of desires (directive representations) is determined by what they have the function to bring about, and the content of beliefs (descriptive representations) is then explained partly in terms of the content of desires.[57] Another theory that emphasizes the use of representations, and which is probably the most influential of all teleological accounts, is Ruth Millikan's "biosemantics" (Millikan 1984, 1989, 2004, 2017).

The core of Millikan's biosemantics consists of two claims. The first is that all representations are, at bottom, messages sent from a producer to one or more "consumers." In other words, representations always stand midway between (i) a producer system that is supposed to generate them and (ii) one or more consumer systems that are supposed to respond to them in specific ways. According to Millikan, these systems must be designed to cooperate with each other, either by natural selection or by a process of individual learning. In the case of the toad, the producer would be the toad's visual system, and the consumer its prey-catching system (i.e., the collection of mechanisms that produce snapping behavior in response to states of T5-2 activation).

The second core claim of Millikan's theory can, to a first approximation, be put as follows: every (descriptive) representation belongs to a set of interrelated representations, and the representations of this set must correspond to, or "map onto," certain other (usually external) states in a systematic way to enable the consumer to perform its functions (its "proper functions," in Millikan's terminology).[58] The states that the representations are supposed to map onto are, of course, the represented states of affairs, that is, the contents of these representations. Taking the two core claims together, we get (what I call) *basic biosemantics (BB)*:[59]

(BB) R_i is a descriptive representation with the content p_j iff

　　i.　R_i stands midway between a producer P and a consumer C;

　　ii.　R_i belongs to a set of interrelated states $R_1, \ldots R_n$ (which all stand midway between P and C), such that the states $R_1, \ldots, R_n$ must map onto certain

---

[57] See, for example, Papineau (1993, 55–71; 1998). For a more detailed presentation and discussion of Papineau's theory, see Schulte and Neander (2022, sec. 3.3).

[58] This is only one part of Millikan's theory. For her account of directive ("desire-like") representations, see Millikan (1984, 96–102; 2004, 191–201).

[59] Cf. Millikan (1984, 96–102; 1989, 283–290; 2004, 71–86).

other states $p_1, \ldots, p_n$ in a systematic way in order to enable C to perform its functions; and

iii. R_i must map onto p_j in order to enable C to perform its functions.

In order to transform BB into biosemantics proper, we would need to add two things, namely (a) that, strictly speaking, a correspondence between representation and represented state of affairs is not necessary for the consumer to perform its functions, but only for the consumer to perform its functions "in the Normal way" (Millikan 1984, 100), and (b) that a certain kind of relation-preserving "isomorphism" or "homomorphism" must exist between the set of representations and the set of represented states of affairs (Millikan 2004, chap. 6; 2021).[60] However, since these aspects of biosemantics are not crucial to understanding the central idea of the theory, I will leave them to one side here.

To get clearer about BB, let us apply it to the toad case. As we have already seen, T5-2+ states satisfy condition (i). What about condition (ii)? First, does each T5-2+ state belong to an appropriate "set of interrelated states $R_1, \ldots, R_n$"? The answer is "yes", but what this set is depends on the details of the case. In a simple (and very unrealistic) version of the scenario, the toad's visual system responds to small, dark, moving objects anywhere in its visual field by generating the same type of T5-2+ state, which triggers an (undirected) snapping reaction. Even in this case, Millikan would say that the second condition is fulfilled, since the representational vehicles (the Rs) in this case are really complexes consisting of a state of T5-2 activation, a time and a location (cf. Millikan 1984, 116), so that any particular complex of *T5-2+ occurring at time t in location l* is a member of a large set of interrelated vehicles (comprising many T5-2+ states occurring at different times in different locations). In a more realistic case, however, the toad's visual system activates different populations of T5-2 neurons depending on where in the visual field the small, dark, moving object appears (see Neander 2017, 109–115), so that there is an even richer set of interrelated R-states to which each particular state of T5-2 activation belongs.

To avoid unnecessary complications, let us stick to the simple version of the example and consider the second part of condition (ii). In order to determine what the T5-2+ states have to correspond to in order to enable the consumer to fulfill its proper functions, we first have to identify the proper functions of their consumer, that is, of the prey-catching mechanism that responds to T5-2+ states by generating snapping behavior. Plausibly, a central function of this mechanism is to provide the toad with food, that is, with nutritious objects (since this is,

---

[60] This relation-preserving "isomorphism" is, in effect, a relation of second-order similarity, but *not* the kind of second-order similarity that O'Brien and Opie (2004) call "structural resemblance" (see Section 4.3).

surely, what the mechanism was selected for). Now, it is clear that in order for the prey-catching mechanism to fulfill this function, states of the form *T5-2+ occurring at time t and in location l* must correspond to ("map onto") states of the form *nutritious object present at time t in location l*. Hence, the content of T5-2+ states is *a nutritious object is present at time t in location l*, or more simply, *toad food here now* (cf. Millikan 1991, 163).

Due to its prominence, Millikan's biosemantics has been the target of many criticisms; of these, I will only mention three. First, some authors have questioned whether the content ascriptions entailed by biosemantics (e.g., *toad food here now* for the toad's T5-2+ states) are plausible (Pietroski 1992) or whether they are consistent with mainstream information-processing theories of cognition (Neander 2006; Schulte 2012). Secondly, Neander (1995) has argued that the content ascriptions actually entailed by biosemantics are much more specific than Millikan acknowledges (e.g., *here is toad food that is not infected, not located in the vicinity of crows, etc.* for the toad's T5-2+ states) and that this consequence is untenable (for a reply, see Millikan 2004, 85–86). Thirdly, Millikan's theory has been criticized as "overly liberal," since it attributes contentful states to very simple organisms (see Section 8.2 for discussion).

Naturally, this overview of teleological accounts of content only provides a glimpse of the full theoretical landscape. In addition to the theories of Neander and Millikan, and the other accounts mentioned briefly in passing, there are the "hybrid" (partly input-, partly output-oriented) theories proposed by Price (2001) and Shea (2007), Ryder's (2004) "SINBAD neurosemantics," Shea's (2018) influential "varitel semantics," Martínez's (2013) "homeostatic cluster" view and Artiga's (2021) "e-teleosemantics." And the number of teleological accounts on offer is still growing.

Despite the evident popularity of the teleosemantic approach, some of its critics have long argued that it is fundamentally flawed. General problems that have been raised for teleosemantics include, for example, indeterminacy worries and the problem of content epiphenomenalism (see Section 4.3), but the most famous challenge for the teleosemantic approach is, without a doubt, the Swampman objection (see, e.g., Braddon-Mitchell and Jackson 2007, 211–212).[61] Swampman is a hypothetical creature that comes into being purely by accident when lightning strikes a dead tree in a swamp. By a cosmic coincidence, Swampman is an intrinsic duplicate of Donald Davidson; consequently, he talks and behaves just like Davidson would talk and behave in every situation. But since Swampman (right after his formation) has neither an

---

[61] The Swampman thought experiment is originally due to Davidson (1987, 443), but he does not use it to argue against teleosemantics.

evolutionary history nor a history of individual learning, his neural structures cannot have any etiological functions. Hence, teleosemantic theories are committed to deny that Swampman has beliefs, desires or any other representational states. This is supposed to be a *reductio* of the teleological approach.

Proponents of teleosemantics have reacted differently to this problem. Most have argued that pre-theoretic intuitions about Swampman's mental states are wholly irrelevant to teleosemantics, because teleosemantic accounts are not to be understood as conceptual analyses of mental concepts, but rather as a posteriori, real-nature theories akin to "water = H_2O" (Millikan 1996; Neander 1996). Other theorists have pointed out that teleosemanticists can adopt a non-etiological notion of function and avoid the Swampman problem altogether (Nanay 2014). And there are still further options available (see, e.g., Papineau 2001, 2022; see also Schulte 2020 for discussion).

All in all, it seems that neither the Swampman problem nor the other general objections have been able to seriously undermine the teleosemantic research program.

4.5 Conceptual Role Semantics

The basic idea of *conceptual roles semantics* (CRS) can be described as follows: the content of a representation R is determined by the cognitive role it plays within a system. Standard versions of CRS construe cognitive roles as causal roles (or, equivalently, as functional roles in the sense of classical functionalism). These theories, which are also described as variants of "causal role" or "functional role semantics," offer fully naturalistic accounts of content (Field 1977; Harman 1982; Block 1986). However, it should be noted that there are other versions of CRS that are not naturalistic in this sense (e.g., Brandom 1994).[62] .

A version of CRS that is of special interest in the present context is Ned Block's (1986) "two-factor" account. This account is naturalistic, but unlike all (or nearly all) other naturalistic theories of content/representation discussed in this section, it is based on a (moderate) Fregean conception of content (see Section 2.3). According to this conception, representations possess a primary kind of content, which is Fregean, and a secondary, derivative kind of content, which is non-Fregean (referential).[63] (These two kinds of content are, of course, the eponymous "two factors.")

Block's main thesis is that the primary, Fregean content of a representation R is determined by R's conceptual role. The conceptual role of R is its "total

---

[62] For a useful survey of different versions of CRS, see Whiting (2022).

[63] Note, however, that this is my terminology, not Block's.

causal role, abstractly described" (Block 1986, 628). More precisely, it is R's causal role when we "[abstract] away from all causal relations except the ones that mediate inferences, inductive or deductive, decision making, and the like" (Block 1986, 628). What is important is that Block construes these roles as "short-armed" functional roles that "stop roughly at the skin," with "proximal stimuli" as inputs and "bodily movements" as outputs (Block 1986, 363).[64] Hence, on Block's view, the Fregean content of mental representations is *narrow*.

Their non-Fregean (referential) content, by contrast, is construed as *broad content*. Block suggests that it is determined by a representation's narrow content together with contextual factors. How this works in detail is left open, but Block offers some suggestive examples that illustrate the general idea. Take the Twin Earth scenario from Section 3.2 (Block discusses the original Twin Earth example, but the differences do not matter). In this scenario, the beliefs of Abigail and Twin Abigail have the same narrow (Fregean) content, because the conceptual role of their respective DIAMOND concepts is identical. This follows from the fact that conceptual roles are understood as short-armed roles, together with the fact that Abigail and Twin Abigail are intrinsic duplicates of each other. However, the broad (non-Fregean) content of their beliefs is different: Abigail's DIAMOND concept refers to diamonds, Twin Abigail's DIAMOND concept refers to twin diamonds. Or, to put it another way, in the Earth environment, a concept with the conceptual role that is shared by Abigail's and Twin Abigail's DIAMOND concept picks out diamonds as the referent; in a Twin Earth environment, such a concept picks out twin diamonds as the referent. This is why we can say that a representation's broad content is determined by its narrow content together with the context or (equivalently) that a representation's narrow content determines a function from contexts to broad contents (Block 1986, 644).

There are several respects in which Block's proposal is attractive, but it also faces a number of problems. One major problem that Block himself mentions is this: How exactly are conceptual roles individuated? Suppose that the TIGER concepts of Laurel and Hardy are the same, except for the fact that Laurel infers "x is dangerous" from "x is a tiger," while Hardy does not. Do their TIGER concepts have the same conceptual role or not? In general, which differences in causal/inferential dispositions make it the case that two representations count as having different conceptual roles (and thus different Fregean contents) and which do not? This question is difficult to answer. On the one hand, it seems

---

[64] In this respect, Block's account differs fundamentally from Gilbert Harman's "single-factor" version of CRS, which construes conceptual roles as world-involving, "long-armed" functional roles (Harman 1982).

that proponents of CRS cannot claim that *all* differences count, since this would entail a radical form of holism, which makes it virtually impossible for two people to share representations with the same narrow content. On the other hand, it is hard to see how the proponents of CRS can draw a principled (and noncircular) distinction between those causal/inferential differences that count and those that do not.

Another worry concerns Block's notion of narrow content. Is this narrow content really a type of *content*, given that (according to Block) a representation's narrow content determines its referent or truth-conditions only together with the context? Block responds that this is a "merely verbal" issue (Block 1986, 626). While defending his choice of words, he concedes that we could substitute the phrase "narrow determinant of meaning" for the term "narrow content" (Block 1986, 627). However, critics might worry that this trivializes the notion of narrow content.

Finally, like all other naturalistic theories of content, CRS accounts are subject to indeterminacy worries (see, e.g., Kripke 1982; cf. Whiting 2022 for discussion). Block does not address these worries explicitly, and his theory sketch is not detailed enough to indicate how he intends to deal with them.

For these and other reasons, CRS has not been very popular among semantic naturalizers in recent decades. However, there has been some revival of interest in the approach, as we shall see in Section 8.2.

5 Theories of Mental Content II: Interpretationism and Intentional Stance Theory

The group of theories that we now turn to occupies a middle ground between strong realism about content on the one hand and content eliminativism on the other. Proponents of these "middle ground" theories reject strong realism because they do not think of content properties as "ontologically robust" properties of internal states that must either be explained naturalistically (see Section 4) or non-naturalistically (see Section 6) or taken as primitive. And they oppose eliminativism because they accept content ascriptions as true.

"Middle ground" theories range from different versions of interpretationism proposed by David Lewis (1974), Donald Davidson (1984) and the early Robert Cummins (1989) to Frances Egan's (2014) "content pragmatism."[65] Since the main commonality of these theories is a negative feature (their opposition to both strong realism and eliminativism), it is no surprise that they form a very heterogeneous group. Hence, I will not try to provide a systematic survey of

---

[65] Two further "middle ground" proposals are Mark Sprevak's (2013) "fictionalism" and Dimitri Coelho Mollo's (2022) "deflationary realism."

these theories here. Instead, I will focus on one particular proposal: Daniel Dennett's *intentional stance theory* (Dennett 1971, 1981/1987, 2009), which is by far the most influential theory of this type, both inside and outside of philosophy.

Dennett starts with the observation that we adopt different attitudes or "stances" when we are trying to predict the behavior of objects we encounter in daily life (Dennett 1981/1987, 16–21; 2009, 339–341). Toward some objects, for example stones, mountains or puddles of water, we adopt the *physical stance*: we use the laws of "folk physics" – or, if we are very serious about it, physical science – to predict how these objects will behave in the near future. Toward other objects, we adopt the *design stance*. When we encounter an alarm clock, for instance, we assume that it was designed for a certain purpose and predict that it will go off in the morning at 7:00 a.m. if we press its buttons in a certain order. Finally, there are some objects toward which we adopt the *intentional stance*. This includes other human beings but also many animals and some complex artificial systems (like chess computers or autonomous robots). Very roughly, we predict the behavior of each of these objects by treating it as a "rational agent": we ascribe to it the beliefs and desires it "ought to have, given its place in the world and its purpose" and predict that it will "act to further its goals in the light of its beliefs" (Dennett 1981/1987, 17; cf. also Dennett 2009, 341).

The fact that we are able to take these different stances toward objects is highly significant. Predicting the behavior of an alarm clock from the physical stance is surely possible but would involve an enormous amount of time-consuming measurements and calculations, so we are clearly better off using the design stance. Moreover, predicting the behavior of humans, animals or even chess computers from the physical stance, while possible in principle (at least according to Dennett), is plainly impossible in practice. So, it seems that the intentional stance is indispensable for predicting the behavior of these special kinds of entities.

So far, Dennett's story about the three stances is acceptable to theorists of very different stripes, including most of the theorists discussed in Section 4. Let us now consider the crucial step that turns this story into a distinctive account of contentful mental states. Dennett defines a "true believer" as a system that has beliefs, desires and other representational states and puts forward the following thesis: "*What it is* to be a true believer is to be an *intentional system*, a system whose behavior is reliably and voluminously predictable via the intentional strategy" (Dennett 1981/1987, 15). In other words, Dennett maintains that a system S has states with representational content iff we are able to predict S's behavior "reliably and voluminously" by adopting the intentional stance

toward S. This means, among other things, that a representational characterization of S entails no specific claims about S's internal organization (i.e., about the
internal structures that bring about S's behavior).

Some have interpreted Dennett's view as a form of instrumentalism, according to which beliefs, desires and other representational states are mere "useful
fictions" that allow us to predict behavior. But Dennett is very clear (at least in
his later writings) that this is not his view. He holds that belief ascriptions, for
example, are literally true of a system S if S's behavior can be predicted (to
a significant extent) from the intentional stance and that there is an objective fact
of the matter about whether S fulfills this condition. It is just that this objective
fact of the matter has nothing to do with the particular internal organization of
S.[66] Hence, Dennett's position is best described as a "weak" or "mild" form of
realism about representational states (Dennett 1981/1987, 28; 1991/1998).

The realist character of Dennett's theory is well illustrated by a thought
experiment that he discusses in Dennett (1981/1987, 25–8). Suppose there is
a race of hyperintelligent Martians who are able to make reliable predictions
about human behavior from the physical stance. These Martians do not need to
adopt the intentional stance toward us in order to predict what we will do, so are
they missing something if they never learn to characterize us (and our behavior)
in representational terms? Dennett's answer is: yes, they *are* missing something,
namely "the *patterns* in human behavior that are describable from the intentional stance" (Dennett 1981/1987, 25). These patterns are perfectly objective
high-level features of reality or, as Dennett also puts it, "real patterns" (for an in-
depth discussion of this notion, see Dennett 1991/1998).

One objection that is often raised against Dennett's theory is that it is far too
liberal. Isn't it true for almost anything that we can predict its behavior via the
intentional strategy? Prima facie, it may seem that even the "behavior" of
a university lectern that always remains in one and the same place can be
explained by treating it as an intentional system that believes that it is "currently
located at the center of the civilized world" and desires "above all else to remain
at that center" (Dennett 1981/1987, 23). In reply to this objection, Dennett
maintains that the lectern does not qualify as a "true believer" since, in this case,
"we get no predictive power from [the intentional strategy] that we did not
antecedently have" (Dennett 1981/1987, 23). Taking the intentional stance

---

[66] Note that Dennett's view is compatible with a scenario in which all systems whose behavior can
be reliably and voluminously predicted from the intentional stance also share, as a matter of
empirical fact, a certain type of internal organization. Dennett's claim is merely that, even in such
a scenario, belief ascriptions would not be true of these systems in virtue of the fact that they have
a certain internal organization but in virtue of the fact that they possess certain behavioral
dispositions.

toward the lectern does not enable us to predict anything that we could not also (and more easily) predict from the physical stance. Apparently, a system's behavior only counts as being "reliably and voluminously predictable via the intentional strategy" if adopting this strategy is associated with a *gain* in predictive power.

Still, Dennett admits that the intentional strategy does lead to (small, but non-zero) increases in predictive power when it comes to the behavior of other "simple" systems – for instance, thermostats, clams and plants (Dennett 1981/1987, 22; 2009, 342). According to Dennett, we cannot say categorically that these systems lack representational states; instead, he maintains that they "fall on a continuum of cases of legitimate attributions [of representational states; PS], with no theoretically motivated threshold distinguishing the 'literal' from the 'metaphorical'" (Dennett 2009, 343). This is an interesting position but one that will seem unacceptable to staunch opponents of representational liberalism (see Section 8.2 for discussion).

Another very influential objection to Dennett's theory is the *Blockhead objection* (see, e.g., Braddon-Mitchell and Jackson 2007, 162–163). In the Blockhead thought experiment (originally proposed by Block 1978, 294–295; 1981, 19–25), we are asked to imagine a futuristic computer (the "Blockhead") that is capable of engaging in written exchanges with a human interlocutor, as long as the whole conversation has some finite length – say, a length of 20,000 characters at most. The computer's responses to its interlocutor are always coherent and sensible, so it passes the famous "Turing test" with flying colors. However, as it turns out, the *mechanism* that underlies the computer's capacity for conversation is highly unusual. The first thing to note is that the computer has access to a massive database that contains all sensible conversations that do not exceed a limit of 20,000 characters. These conversations are called "sensible strings" (Block 1981, 19), and their number is vast but finite. Secondly, the program running on the computer is exceedingly simple: after receiving a new input from the interlocutor, it compares the whole of the conversation so far (the "current string") to the strings in its database, randomly selects one of the strings that matches with the current string and generates an output by reproducing the answer contained in the selected string. In other words, the computer produces its answers by consulting a "giant look-up table" (Dennett 2009, 347).

Now, it seems clear that this computer should *not* be credited with beliefs and desires, even though its verbal behavior can be predicted quite successfully from the intentional stance (as successfully as the verbal behavior of human beings, if the only data we have are their previous messages in a time-limited online conversation). Prima facie, this is a fundamental problem for Dennett's theory, and it is exacerbated by further variants of the thought experiment, which involve "Blockheads" that are also able to generate seemingly intelligent *nonverbal* behavior (see, e.g., Braddon-Mitchell and Jackson 2007, 116–119). In all these cases, it seems that the system in question does not qualify as having beliefs and desires because it has the wrong kind of internal organization – an intuitive verdict that is plainly inconsistent with Dennett's account (for a reply, see Dennett 2009, 347–348).

Despite these problems, however, Dennett's account remains one of the most attractive "middle ground" theories currently on offer.

6 Theories of Mental Content III: The Phenomenal Intentionality Approach

Another alternative to semantic naturalism, besides interpretationism and the intentional stance theory, is the *phenomenal intentionality approach*, which has become increasingly popular in recent decades (Searle 1983; Loar 2003; Strawson 2008; Graham, Horgan and Tienson 2017; Mendelovici 2018). The basic idea of this approach has already been alluded to in Sections 2.4 and 3.1: it is the idea that mental content can be explained in terms of phenomenal consciousness or, in other words, that the content properties of mental states can be explained in terms of the phenomenal properties of mental states.

As these initial remarks already indicate, I use the term "phenomenal intentionality approach" (or "PIA," for short) in a sense that is slightly narrower than the sense in which some other theorists use it (e.g., Bourget and Mendelovici 2019). In my terminology, a theory qualifies as a version of PIA only if it includes the claim that content properties can be constitutively explained by appealing to phenomenal properties, either because content properties are grounded in phenomenal properties or because a reductive identification of content properties with phenomenal properties is possible.[67] Furthermore, I will mostly ignore the less common "reductive identification" view for the sake of simplicity.

Given these clarifications, we can say that there are two main strands of PIA: strong PIA and moderate PIA (modeled after "strong PIT" and "moderate PIT" in Bourget and Mendelovici 2019, sec. 2.2). According to strong PIA, all contentful mental states are such that their content is (fully) grounded in their

---

[67] Hence, as I use the term, the "phenomenal intentionality approach" includes only those theories that Bourget and Mendelovici (2019) describe as "reductive" phenomenal intentionality theories. Consequently, it does not include (a) theories that identify phenomenal properties with content properties, but do not maintain that phenomenal descriptions of these properties are more fundamental than descriptions in terms of content (i.e., identity theories that do not "reduce" content properties to phenomenal properties), and (b) "weak" phenomenal intentionality theories that merely say that some states with content properties also have phenomenal properties (as I would put it).

own phenomenal character.[68] According to moderate PIA, all contentful mental states are such that *either* (a) their content is (fully) grounded in their own phenomenal character *or* (b) their content is at least partly grounded in the phenomenal character of other mental states (Searle 1983; Loar 2003; Graham, Horgan and Tienson 2017). The second view is more moderate because it allows for the possibility that there are some genuinely contentful states, for example standing beliefs, that are not themselves phenomenally conscious but get their content from standing in certain relations to other states that *are* phenomenally conscious. Prima facie, this is an attractive feature of the view, and it is the reason why moderate PIA is favored by most proponents of the phenomenal intentionality approach.

Typically, proponents of both versions of PIA assume that phenomenal properties cannot, in turn, be explained with the resources of naturalistic theories of content (i.e., in terms of causation, probabilistic dependence, structural similarity or the like). In other words, they defend *non-naturalistic* PIA theories. These variants of (strong or moderate) PIA are especially interesting, since they constitute genuine theoretical alternatives to naturalistic accounts. On the other hand, they are also especially controversial, since they seem to entail *property dualism*, the view that phenomenal properties are ontologically independent of physical properties (or, at least, something that is close to this view).[69]

Let us now turn to the reasons that have been offered in support of the phenomenal intentionality approach. To provide some initial motivation for their position, proponents of PIA often point to the apparent *inseparability* of phenomenal character and representational content (see especially Horgan and Tienson 2002; Graham, Horgan and Tienson 2017). Suppose that you have a visual experience E, which represents that three small blue spheres are located on top of a big red cube. This experience has a particular phenomenal character. Now, can there be another experience with exactly the same phenomenal character as E but with a different representational content? Intuitively, it is hard to see how this could be possible. If a visual experience has the very same

---

[68] Roughly speaking, this is the position that Mendelovici (2018) advocates, although she holds a "reductive identity" version of it, rather than a grounding version.

[69] By saying that phenomenal properties are "ontologically independent" of physical properties, I mean that they are neither identical with nor grounded in (constituted by) physical properties. If proponents of non-naturalistic PIA theories want to avoid a dualism of this kind, they have to commit themselves to the following hypothesis: phenomenal properties are grounded in (or identical with) physical properties that are not available as explanatory resources for current naturalistic theories of content, either because these properties are still wholly unknown to us or because our understanding of them is so incomplete that we are unable to grasp how they are connected to representational properties. This is what I mean by a view that is "close" to property dualism.

phenomenal character as E, it cannot represent (say) that two big blue spheres are located in front of a small red cube or that there are four green pyramids arranged in a row. E's representational content appears to be *inseparable* from its phenomenal character; and the same holds, at least prima facie, for all other sensory-perceptual states. Moreover, if propositional attitudes (beliefs, desires, etc.) have phenomenal character, as many proponents of PIA argue,[70] then this line of argument can be extended to them, too.

However, this intuitive consideration is not enough to support PIA. Even if it succeeds, it only establishes that representational content and phenomenal character are not ontologically independent of each other, not that representational content is grounded in phenomenal character. A fortiori, the argument does not give us any reason to accept a non-naturalistic version of PIA.

Other arguments in the literature do aim to provide support for a non-naturalistic version of PIA. One of them is the *argument from content determinacy* (Strawson 2008; Horgan and Graham 2012).[71] Terry Horgan and George Graham (henceforth H&G) provide a detailed version of this argument that has three main steps. They start from the common-sense view that our thoughts, beliefs and perceptual states have determinate content and that it is immediately obvious to us that they do. When I think "there's a rabbit," then I know that my thought refers to a rabbit and not to an undetached rabbit part;[72] when I have a visual perception of a red cube, then I know that my perceptual state represents a three-dimensional object in my environment and not a two-dimensional retinal image or a series of signals in my optic nerve (see Section 4.1); and so on.

In a second step, H&G argue that naturalistic theories of content are unable to account for the determinacy of representational content. Naturalistic theories try to explain content in terms of publicly accessible relations between internal states and the environment, for example in terms of causal relations, probabilistic relations or functional relationships. However, according to H&G, none of these "naturalistic connections" (or "R-mappings") seems capable of yielding determinate contents because, "[in] general, if there is one R-mapping from a creature's inner states to objects and/or kinds in the creature's environment, then there are apt to be numerous other such R-mappings as well" (Horgan and Graham 2012, 327).

In a third step, H&G contend that PIA can account for the determinacy of mental content. If mental content is grounded in phenomenal character, then

---

[70] This position is known as the "cognitive phenomenology view."

[71] Neither Strawson nor Horgan and Graham would describe their theories as "non-naturalistic," but it is clear that both theories count as non-naturalistic in my sense of the term.

[72] This is a reference to W. V. O. Quine's famous "Gavagai" example (cf. Quine 1960, chap. 2).

mental content is determinate, since phenomenal character is not only "inherently intentional, but . . . also inherently *determinately* intentional" (Horgan and Graham 2012, 338). Hence, the determinacy of mental content supports a non-naturalistic version of PIA over naturalistic accounts of content.

A number of objections can be raised against the argument from content determinacy. First, it rests on the controversial assumption that no naturalistic theory of content will ever be able to account for the determinacy of mental content. Secondly, it can be objected that the explanation of content determinacy offered by PIA is, in effect, an *obscurum per obscurius* explanation – an explanation of something mysterious by something even more mysterious. As Neander remarks in her reply to Galen Strawson, a PIA-style explanation of content determinacy "might strike us as a magic theory," a theory that boils down to the claim "that, when we add consciousness to the mix, *pff*!" (Neander 2017, 5). Thirdly, the PIA-style explanation of content determinacy (especially as it is spelled out by H&G and Strawson) is strangely disconnected from facts about neural information-processing, so that it almost seems like a lucky accident that, for example, most perceptual states which determinately represent that p also normally co-vary with the state that p.

Furthermore, there are general objections that are directed against PIA itself and against non-naturalistic versions of PIA in particular. First, standard versions of PIA presuppose a traditional conception of phenomenal consciousness that identifies the phenomenal character of a mental state with a property that is "ineffable," "intrinsic," "private" and "directly or immediately apprehensible in consciousness" (Dennett 1988/1997, 622) – a conception that has been severely criticized by many authors (Dennett 1988/1997; Frankish 2016). Secondly, as I have already pointed out, non-naturalistic versions of PIA entail a form of property dualism, which brings with it a whole range of familiar metaphysical and epistemological problems.

7 Skepticism about Content: Anti-representationalist Approaches

All the approaches we have discussed so far start from the common assumption that mental content is a real and important phenomenon and then go on to offer different accounts of that phenomenon – accounts that are either strongly or at least weakly realist. The "anti-representationalist" approaches that we turn to in this section, by contrast, question this common assumption: their proponents adopt a skeptical attitude toward either the existence or the significance of contentful, representational states.

Given this characterization, the label "anti-representationalism" applies to a number of substantively different approaches, including Stephen Stich's (1983) "syntacticism," Anthony Chemero's (2009) "radical embodied cognition" view, the "radical enactivism" of Daniel Hutto and Erik Myin (2013, 2017) and Alexander Rosenberg's (2014) "disenchanted naturalism." Since "anti-representationalism" is such a broad category, I will start by clarifying different ways in which an approach can be anti-representationalist before I examine one particular account in more detail.[73]

First, some anti-representationalists defend content eliminativism (see Section 3.1): they deny that there are such things as representations (i.e., contentful states). A good example of a theorist of this stripe is Rosenberg (2014). Other anti-representationalists only deny that representations can play a genuine role in explanations of behavior or, more precisely, that they can play such a role qua representations (i.e., in virtue of instantiating content properties). Chemero (2009), for instance, is very clear that he only aims to establish that "our best explanations of cognitive systems will not involve representations" (Chemero 2009, 67) and not that representations do not exist.

Secondly, some versions of anti-representationalism are fully general, denying the existence or explanatory relevance of *all* kinds of mental representations, while others are more restricted in scope. Again, Rosenberg's (2014) "disenchanted naturalism" is a good example of the first type of view: Rosenberg holds a fully general version of anti-representationalism, according to which there are no representational states of any kind. This contrasts, for example, with the anti-representationalist position of Hutto and Myin (2013, 2017), who claim that no representations are involved in cognitive processes of nonlinguistic animals but accept that language-using creatures do have representational states.

Let us take a closer look at the position of Hutto and Myin (henceforth H&M). They call their approach "Radical Enactive (or Embodied) Cognition" or "REC" and propose it as an alternative to the traditional view that cognition necessarily involves content (Hutto and Myin 2013, ix–xii). In contrast to this traditional view, H&M maintain that "the great bulk of world-directed, action-guiding cognition" (Hutto and Myin 2013, 82), including perception and all other cognitive processes found in nonlinguistic subjects, does not involve any contentful states (representations). Instead, such

---

[73] This list does not contain the "eliminativism" of Paul and Patricia Churchland, because their view is only directed against the propositional attitudes of folk psychology. With respect to content/representations in general, the Churchlands are *not* eliminativists (see Churchland and Churchland 1983; Churchland 2012).

processes exhibit a type of "intentional directedness that is not contentful" (Hutto and Myin 2013, 82).

There are several ways in which H&M motivate their position. I will focus on one motivation that is of particular interest in the context of this Element: the "hard problem of content" (Hutto and Myin 2013, chap. 4; see also Hutto and Satne 2015). They start from the observation that there is a scientifically respectable notion of information, "information-as-covariance," according to which one state carries information about another "iff the occurrence of these states of affairs covary lawfully, or reliably enough" (Hutto and Myin 2013, 66). As they rightly point out, information (in this sense) is clearly different from representational content: tree rings, columns of smoke and quail tracks carry information about other states of affairs without representing them (see Section 4.2).

Moreover, according to H&M, bringing in other naturalistically respectable properties of nonlinguistic cognitive systems (either in addition to or instead of information) does not help either. At this point in the argument, H&M concentrate their attention on (standard) teleological theories, which are "the clear front-runners among existing naturalistic proposals" (Hutto and Myin 2013, 75). These theories account for content in terms of etiological functions, which are taken to be grounded in selectional processes (see Section 4.4). Drawing on arguments by Jerry Fodor, H&M maintain that selectional processes – and, *ipso facto*, etiological functions – are too coarse-grained to provide sufficient conditions for content. Fodor (1990a) famously argues that, because of the coarse-grained, "extensional" character of selection, teleological theories cannot provide content ascriptions that differentiate between locally co-instantiated properties. To return to the toad example from Section 4.4, if the properties of being a fly, being a small, dark, moving object and being toad food are co-instantiated in the toad's local environment, then teleological theories (allegedly) entail that the content of the toad's T5-2+ states is indeterminate between *a fly is present, a small, dark, moving object is present* and *toad food is present*. In a nutshell, this is because "Darwin cares how many flies you eat, but not what description you eat them under" (Fodor 1990a, 73; quoted in Hutto and Satne 2015, 531; see also Hutto and Myin 2013, 79–80).

According to H&M, all of this is correct, but it does not mean that teleosemantic theories are worthless: while they fail as accounts of representational content, they offer very promising analyses of a "noncontentful, nonrepresentational" form of intentionality that H&M call "Ur-intentionality" (Hutto and Myin 2017, 95; see also Hutto and Satne 2015). This Ur-intentionality is a "natural involvement relation"[74] that is present in all cases where we have an organism that can react appropriately to objects and states in its environment and where such reactions are mediated by the organism's sensitive responses to "natural signs" of these environmental objects/states (Hutto and Myin 2013, 81). When teleosemantics is reconceived in this way as an account of Ur-intentionality, it becomes "teleosemiotics" (Hutto and Myin 2013, 78). Hence, H&M combine their negative claim that nonlinguistic creatures do not possess representations with the positive claim that they do exhibit a form of basic intentionality (i.e., Ur-intentionality). They hold, furthermore, that this positive claim is important as a basis for explaining "[linguistically] grounded beliefs and judgments," which are genuinely contentful (Hutto and Myin 2013, 82; Hutto and Satne 2015).

This is, without a doubt, an ambitious anti-representationalist proposal. But how convincing is it? First, one might take issue with the "hard problem of content," which is one of the main considerations H&M offer in support of their brand of radical enactivism. For instance, Fodor's (1990a) argument against teleosemantics that H&M rely on seems to be seriously flawed because (a) etiological analyses of functions rely on the notion of "selection for," which is *not* "extensional" in Fodor's sense (see Sterelny 1990, 125–127; Millikan 1991), and (b) teleosemantic theories can draw on other resources in addition to biological functions to reduce or eliminate indeterminacies, so functional indeterminacies do not necessarily carry over to teleosemantic contents (see, e.g., Neander's appeal to a causal notion of a "response" and Millikan's appeal to systematic mapping relations).[75] In fact, the theories of Millikan and Neander presented in Section 4.4 demonstrate convincingly that teleological theories *can* provide content ascriptions that differentiate between locally co-instantiated properties. Of course, it can be questioned whether it is possible to construct a teleosemantic theory that manages to resolve *all* indeterminacy problems; but neither Fodor nor H&M have provided any principled reason to believe that this is impossible. Finally, it can be argued that some degree of content indeterminacy is perfectly acceptable, so that a teleosemantic theory does not even have to resolve all indeterminacy problems in order to be viable (for a sophisticated defense of this position, see Bergman 2023). All these considerations suggest that the "hard problem of content" is less serious than H&M make it out to be.

Secondly, another point of controversy concerns H&M's positive claim that nonlinguistic creatures exhibit a form of contentless Ur-intentionality. By

---

[74] This term, borrowed from Godfrey-Smith (2006, 60), is frequently used by H&M to characterize Ur-intentionality.
[75] See also Mann and Pain (2022b, 28–37), who make this point with respect to Millikan's biosemantics.

introducing the notion of Ur-intentionality, H&M seek to overthrow "neo-Brentanism," the traditional view that equates intentionality with content (Hutto and Myin 2017, chap. 5; cf. Section 2.1). According to H&M, this is a highly significant move, since the notion of Ur-intentionality allows us to "[make] sense of the special kind of target-focused, biologically based normativity exhibited by basic cognition" (Hutto and Myin 2017, 104). Or, as Hutto and Satne (2015, 531) put it, the notion "stays true to the driving idea behind teleosemantics that evolved structures can have a kind of 'specificity' or 'directedness'," while discarding the claim that this is sufficient for content (and truth- or satisfaction-conditions).

However, a skeptic might ask whether much is gained by this move. Suppose, for the sake of the argument, that we accept H&M's negative thesis that non-linguistic creatures do not possess representational states. Obviously, this is perfectly compatible with maintaining that these creatures still have traits with biological functions, including traits (or mechanisms) with "response functions" (cf. Neander 2017, chap. 6). However, if we ascribe to the internal mechanism of some organism the function to produce an effect of type E in response to some condition C, then we already describe it as having some kind of specificity or directedness, as well as some "target-focused, biologically based normativity." When we say, for example, that the pineal gland has the function to produce melatonin in response to the dimming of light, we are saying that it is, in some sense, *directed at* the dimming of light (and, in a different way, at the production of melatonin); and we are ready to describe it as *malfunctioning* if it fails to produce melatonin in response to the dimming of light. This raises the following question: If we accept H&M's claim that cognitive processes in non-linguistic creatures (and basic cognitive processes in general) are not content-involving, why is it not enough to describe these processes as functionally directed and reserve the term "intentionality" for the kind of contentful directedness that is (according to H&M) characteristic of linguistically grounded cognition? What is the point of extending the notion of intentionality, contrary to established philosophical usage, to cover cases of "noncontentful" functional directedness? At the very least, some more arguments are needed to dispel the suspicion that the rejection of neo-Brentanism is a merely terminological move.

Thirdly, it is unclear whether H&M can give a naturalistic account of the content of linguistically grounded judgments and beliefs. If naturalistic resources are insufficient to account for content in the case of nonlinguistic cognition, why are they supposed to be sufficient when it comes to the content of language and belief?[76] This is a significant question, especially in the light of the familiar indeterminacy worries about linguistic content (Quine 1960; Kripke 1982).

---

[76] For a more elaborate version of this objection, see Milkowski (2015).

However, H&M do not say enough about this issue to make it clear what their answer is.

Of course, these objections should not be taken as anything like a final verdict on the proposal of H&M. The debate about radical enactivism and other anti-representationalist approaches is still in its early stages and will surely continue for decades to come.

8 Recent Developments

When looking at new developments in the debate about mental content, one is faced with an embarrassment of riches. Many of these developments have already been discussed, or at least been touched upon, in previous sections, but others have been left unmentioned. In this last section, I will consider two recent trends that are intimately connected and that seem highly significant to me: the "explanatory turn" in the debate about content (Section 8.1) and the renewed interest in (what we have called) the status question (Section 8.2). Notably, both of these trends bear witness to the increasingly close interaction between philosophy of mind and empirical science.

8.1 The Explanatory Turn

The first development I will consider is the increased focus on explanatory issues and especially on the role that content ascriptions (or, equivalently, representational characterizations) play in explanations of psychology and cognitive neuroscience. This increased focus is manifest in the work of many different theorists, from Tyler Burge (2010) and William Ramsey (2007) to Karen Neander (2017), Robert Rupert (2018), Nicholas Shea (2018) and Gualtiero Piccinini (2020).

One area where this development has been particularly important is the debate about *naturalistic* theories of content. Early discussions of naturalistic theories in the 1980s and 1990s often assigned a crucial role to pre-theoretical intuitions: theories were evaluated (at least in part) by how well they captured intuitive judgments about representational content in actual and hypothetical scenarios. In some cases, such an "appeal to intuition" seems warranted, for example, when theories are disqualified because they entail that misrepresentation is impossible, that every physical system has representational states or that content is always massively indeterminate. However, it is rather doubtful whether we should attach much weight to more specific intuitions, for example about the contents of the states that produce prey-catching behavior in toads (Section 4.4), or about the contents of hypothetical creatures like Swampman (Section 4.4), or Pietroski's (1992) "kimu" (a hypothetical species of animals often cited in discussions of teleosemantic theories). Moreover, in many of these cases, there is the danger of an unproductive "clash of intuitions."

The recent shift toward explanatory considerations has changed the situation considerably: it offers a method for evaluating theories of content that rests on a firmer foundation than the intuition-based approach and is also more congenial to the naturalistic worldview. The key idea is to evaluate different theories by how well they can account for the explanatory role that content ascriptions (representational characterizations) play in cognitive science. As Robert Cummins put it early on, a naturalistic account of content/representation is successful only if it "underwrite[s] the explanatory appeals that cognitive theory makes to mental representation" (Cummins 1996, 2). Similar requirements have been endorsed by many other theorists as well (as we will see later in this section). This may be called the "explanatory turn" in the debate about naturalizing content, and it is in my view one of the most important recent developments in that debate.

Importantly, the explanatory turn concerns both the *status* and the *content* question (see Section 4). To recapitulate, the status question asks in virtue of what a state R has content at all (rather than having no content) or, equivalently, in virtue of what a state R counts as representational (rather than nonrepresentational). To see what a shift toward explanatory considerations could mean for this question, we should note first that different answers to it can have very different implications for the distribution of representational states in the world. Roughly speaking, *liberal* answers entail that even certain states of "simpler" organisms (such as nematodes, plants or bacteria) qualify as representations, while *restrictive* answers imply that representational states should only be attributed to more sophisticated creatures.[77] Now, it seems that, from an explanatory perspective, a good criterion for evaluating different answers to the status question is this: an adequate theory of content should only attribute content to states of an organism O (characterize states of O as representational) if such content ascriptions (representational characterizations) can play a role in genuine representational explanations of O's behavior.[78]

Similar considerations apply to the content question – the question concerning the conditions in virtue of which a state R has the content p (rather than some other content q), *given* that it is a representational state. If we formulate

---

[77] Two brief clarificatory remarks. First, I am focusing on organisms here, but, of course, the question can also be extended to machines. Secondly, it should be clear that answers to the status question do not necessarily line up neatly on a "liberality continuum"; it is very well possible for one answer to be at once more liberal *and* more restrictive than another (i.e., to include some organisms that the other excludes and to exclude some organisms that the other includes).

[78] This constraint can be found in the works of many authors; see the references provided later in this section.

a parallel explanatory constraint on answers to this question, it would look like this: an adequate theory of content should only attribute the content p to state R if this content ascription is capable of figuring in genuine representational explanations of O's behavior.[79]

These two constraints raise important questions of interpretation. For the sake of simplicity, I will focus on the explanatory constraint for answers to the status question. Although it often goes unnoticed, two very different versions of this constraint can be found in the literature, and it is important to distinguish between them in order to avoid confusions (see Schulte 2019a).

A *locus classicus* for the first version of the constraint is Tyler Burge's *Origins of Objectivity* (2010).[80] Here is a representative quote:

> In the cases of some sensory states – non-perceptual ones – saying that the states have veridicality conditions [i.e., representational content; PS] would add nothing explanatory to what is known about discriminative sensitivity and the biological function of the sensitivity. ... In such cases, there is no reason to believe that there are representational states. (Burge 2010, 395)

In another passage, Burge applies this principle to a particular case and attacks representational characterizations of a bacterium as inadequate by pointing out that "[everything] in the example can be explained using the notion of biological function ..., normal environmental conditions, and sensory discrimination" (Burge 2010, 300).

As these remarks make clear, Burge seems to assume that representational characterizations play a genuine explanatory role only if the explanations in which these characterizations figure cannot be replaced without loss by explanations couched in wholly nonrepresentational terms (i.e., by explanations that do not employ any representational notions). In other words, representational characterizations of the states of an organism O are adequate only if characterizations of O in representational terms are indispensable for explanatory purposes.

The problem is that this version of the constraint appears to be in conflict with the naturalistic approach to mental content (Artiga 2016, 414–419; Neander 2017, 85, 88).[81] As we have seen, naturalistic theories aim to account for representational content in nonrepresentational, "naturalistically acceptable"

---

[79] This constraint plays a major role in the work of Neander (2006, 2017) and is also adopted by some of her critics (e.g., Green 2017). For another application of this constraint, see Schulte (2012).

[80] Another proponent of the first version of the explanatory constraint is Michael Rescorla (2013, 94–96). Interestingly, Tim van Gelder (1995, 352) also seems to appeal to this version of the constraint in his famous discussion of the Watt governor.

[81] Note that this is not a problem for Burge, who explicitly rejects semantic naturalism.

terms. Such theories are usually construed as reductive accounts that *identify* content properties with (often quite complex) naturalistic properties – or, equivalently, as accounts that say that the very same properties that can be described as content properties can also be characterized in nonrepresentational terms. In light of this, proponents of naturalistic theories seem to be committed to accept that explanations of an organism's behavior that make explicit appeal to representational contents can, at least in principle, be restated in nonrepresentational terms.[82] Hence, from a naturalistic perspective, the fact that the behavior of an organism O can be fully explained in nonrepresentational terms does not show that explanations of O's behavior that make explicit appeal to content properties of O's states are spurious.

Semantic naturalists are thus well advised to adopt another version of the explanatory constraint, and most of them indeed do so (see, e.g., Sterelny 1995; Price 2001, 75; Ramsey 2007, 27; Schulte 2015; Neander 2017, 38–45).[83] This other version comes in several different forms, but what all of them have in common is that they do not focus on representational terms or notions but on representational *properties*.[84] Here is the formulation that seems most appropriate to me:

> A theory of representation is adequate only if the properties it treats as representational are capable of playing a role in genuine representational explanations (i.e., in explanations that are the same kind as paradigmatic representational explanations).[85]

According to this version of the constraint, theories that identify representational properties with naturalistic properties are not ruled out from the outset, since it may well turn out to be the case that naturalistic properties *are* capable of playing the required explanatory role. If naturalistic properties can play this role, then this would mean that it is possible to restate genuine representational explanations in completely nonrepresentational terms but, of course, that is exactly what semantic naturalists do want to claim.

---

[82] See Artiga (2016, 416–418). Moreover, I would contend that a variant of this argument can still be constructed even if the naturalizer's thesis is not interpreted as a claim of property identity but (e.g.) as a universal grounding claim.

[83] For earlier statements of principles that resemble the explanatory constraint, see Dretske (1988, 79–80) and the references given there.

[84] Here is a representative example from the literature: "An account of how representational content is constituted in a class of systems should allow us to show why recognising the *representational properties* of such systems enables better explanations of behaviour than would be available otherwise" (Shea 2018, 29; my emphasis).

[85] Note that this is a very general formulation of the constraint. In my view, a crucial task for semantic naturalists (and other participants in the debate) is to make this constraint more precise by giving a substantive account of the nature of representational explanation.

The second version of the explanatory constraint is thus consistent with the naturalistic approach to content, and it is (in some form or other) at the center of the "explanatory turn" described here. But how does adopting this constraint change the discussion? Simply put, it extends the scope of the naturalization project: in addition to providing a theory of content/representation that answers the status and the content question, the semantic naturalizer now also has to offer a matching account of representational explanations in cognitive science. This account should make it clear how the properties that are described as content properties by their theory can play a genuine role in these explanations.

That is a daunting task, but it is exactly what many contemporary semantic naturalizers – from Cummins (1996) to Neander (2017) and Shea (2018) – are trying to accomplish. In doing this, they are strengthening the connection between the debate about theories of content and the debate about explanations in cognitive science, which (in my estimation) is bound to be stimulating for both fields. Indeed, a lot of interesting work is already being done that is located squarely at the intersection of these two areas (see, e.g., Shagrir 2001; Bechtel 2008; Piccinini 2020, 2022).

Finally, these investigations also bear directly on the more general question of whether any theory of content *can* satisfy the explanatory constraint. Some anti-representationalists have argued, on various grounds, that no theory of content will be able to do so and that contentful states (representations) will thus have no substantive role to play in the explanations of a mature cognitive science (see Section 7). By working out theories of content that satisfy the explanatory constraint, semantic naturalists are, in effect, providing a forceful response to this type of anti-representationalist critique.

8.2 The Status Question Reloaded: Content, Basal Cognition and Predictive Processing

The second remarkable development, which is closely connected to the explanatory turn described in the previous section, is that the status question is receiving increasingly more attention. In earlier discussions of theories of content, the status question has often been overshadowed by the content question and by worries about content indeterminacy in particular, but lately the situation has changed. Interestingly, this change manifests itself in the context of two very different debates: the debate about representation and basal cognition and the debate about the representational commitments of different theories of cognition.

Let us look first at the debate about representation and basal cognition. The question that is at the center of this debate (and that we have already touched on in the previous section) can be put as follows: How far does the realm of representation extend? Does it include insects, spiders and crabs? And what about nematodes, jellyfish, plants and bacteria? The more organisms (or, more generally, systems) an account classifies as representational, the more "liberal" (or less "restrictive") this account is.

It has often been observed that naturalistic theories of content/representation are usually rather liberal, and sometimes very much so. A paradigm example is Millikan's biosemantics (discussed in Section 4.4), which entails that many (and perhaps all) plants and bacteria are representational systems. Consider, for instance, a hormone-regulated defense system that is present in many plants (Vos, Pieterse and van Wees 2013). When herbivores attack the plant, their oral secretions trigger the production of a plant hormone, jasmonic acid (JA), which activates a defense mechanism (e.g., a mechanism for the release of toxic chemicals). In this case, we have a producer (the JA release mechanism) and a consumer (the defense mechanism), as well as a family of interrelated states that stand midway between them (increases of JA at different times). Moreover, these intermediaries have to "map onto" environmental states (the presence of herbivores at different times) if the consumer is to function properly. Hence, Millikan would categorize JA increases as representations of herbivores.

This radical form of liberalism has been attacked by many theorists. Burge (2010), for instance, argues against it on the basis of explanatory considerations (see Section 8.1). However, since Burge's argument seems to rest on the first version of the explanatory constraint, which is incompatible with semantic naturalism, it has been criticized as begging the question against proponents of liberal naturalistic theories like Millikan (see Artiga 2016, 414–419). Other theorists have raised objections against radical liberalism that are broadly similar to Burge's argument but that are best interpreted as drawing on the second version of the explanatory constraint (Sterelny 1995; Ramsey 2007, chap. 4; Schulte 2015; Shea 2018, 213–216). These theorists argue that the properties that are identified as content properties by Millikan's biosemantics and related theories, and that are instantiated by the states of "simple" organisms (e.g., by JA increases in plants), cannot play a role in genuine representational explanations of the behavior of these organisms. Of course, whether this is correct depends on substantive claims about the nature of representational explanations and is thus very much an open question (for discussion, see Artiga 2016; Schulte 2019a; Butlin 2020; Ganson 2020; Arnellos and Moreno 2021).

But suppose that it is correct and that radical liberalism does indeed violate the explanatory constraint. Does that constitute a problem for naturalistic theories of content in general? In Schulte (2015), I argue that this is not the case and that naturalists can easily avoid radical representational liberalism by appealing to the notion of *perceptual constancies*[86] in their account of representation (thus turning a well-known anti-naturalist argument from Burge 2010 on its head).[87] Obviously, this requires that it is possible to give a naturalistic account of perceptual constancies, which is only sketched in Schulte (2015) but developed in detail in Schulte (2021). Other naturalistic strategies for avoiding radical representational liberalism are proposed, for example, by Shea (2018, 213–216), Martínez (2019) and Butlin (2020).[88] This clearly suggests, at the very least, that not all naturalistic accounts of representation have to attribute representational status to states like JA increases in plants.

This brings us to the second debate where the status question has taken center stage: the debate about the representational commitments of different theories of cognition. The crucial question here is always whether the states postulated by a theory T qualify as genuine representations or, equivalently, whether T is a truly representational theory. Ramsey (2007, chap. 4), for instance, argues that many connectionist models, although often stated in representational terms, are not truly representational: the states postulated by these models should not be classified as genuine representations, because they do not play the required explanatory role.

More recently, the same question has been asked for predictive processing (PP) accounts of cognition. According to PP accounts, the brain is an "organ for prediction error minimization" (Kiefer and Hohwy 2018, 2388). Very briefly, the idea is that the brain contains a hierarchical model of causal regularities in the world that comprises (a) estimates of the prior probabilities of various events and (b) estimates of the likelihoods of certain events given the occurrence of other events. Crucially, class (b) includes the likelihoods of various types of sensory stimulation given certain external events. From this model, the brain generates predictions about what will happen in the future, which terminate (at the "bottom level" of the hierarchy) in predictions about sensory inputs. These

---

[86] Very roughly, a perceptual constancy is the ability of a perceptual system to correctly represent a stable property of an object (e.g., the object's size, shape or color) *as* stable despite significant changes in proximal sensory input, due to changes in perceptual conditions. For instance, when I perceive a statue as remaining the same in size while I approach it, despite the fact that the size of the statue's image on my retina changes dramatically in the process, my visual system exhibits size constancy.

[87] For a different account of representational status that also appeals to perceptual constancies, see de Souza Filho (2022).

[88] Furthermore, there are a number of proposals for avoiding radical liberalism that are not formulated within the context of constructing a naturalistic account of representation but which could be adapted for that purpose; see, for example, Beckermann (1988), Sterelny (1995) (a proposal that I draw on in Schulte 2015) and Orlandi (2020).

predictions are then compared to the sensory inputs that the brain actually receives. If the discrepancy between prediction and actual outcome (the "prediction error") is large enough, an error signal is sent up the representational hierarchy. This signal either (i) leads to an adjustment of the prior probabilities and likelihoods at different levels of the hierarchy ("perceptual inference") or (ii) to the initiation of actions suitable to change the sensory input ("active inference"), so that, either way, the prediction error is minimized.[89]

On the face of it, the PP account looks like a representational theory: estimates of prior probabilities and likelihoods, and predictions generated on their basis, all seem to be representational posits. But is this really the case or are such representational characterizations of the theory's posits unjustified? Pawel Gladziejewski (2016) claims that first impressions are *not* deceiving in this case and that the PP account is, in fact, a truly representational theory. He argues that the internal model postulated by the PP account qualifies as a structural representation ("S-representation"): very roughly, (i) states of the internal model correspond to states in the external world, (ii) the causal-probabilistic relationships between states of the internal model correspond to causal-probabilistic relationships between external states and (iii) the causal-probabilistic relationships between states of the internal model and predictions of sensory input states correspond to causal-probabilistic relationships between external states and the sensory input states themselves.[90] Furthermore, Gladziejewski holds that there are good reasons to view structural representations as genuinely representational, that is, as representations that "earn their explanatory keep" (see also Gladziejewski and Milkowski 2017).

However, as in the debate about representation and basal cognition, the question is far from being settled. Some theorists agree with Gladziejewski or argue for the representationalist credentials of the PP account in a different way (see, e.g., Kiefer and Hohwy 2018, who appeal to a version of conceptual/ functional role semantics), while other theorists defend a nonrepresentationalist interpretation of the PP account (e.g., Kirchhoff and Robertson 2018) – and the jury is still out on who is right in this debate.[91]

---

[89] In this simplifying description, I am ignoring the important role that "precision estimates" (roughly, estimates of the reliability of the sensory input) play in the process of prediction error minimization. See Hohwy (2013) and Clark (2016) for detailed discussions of the PP framework and Wiese and Metzinger (2017) for a helpful introduction.

[90] Note that these are *not* structural representations in the sense of O'Brien and Opie (2004), because the second-order similarity obtains in virtue of the *causal* relations that hold between the representational vehicles, rather than in virtue of (what O'Brien and Opie call) "physical" relations between vehicles (see Section 4.3).

[91] For further discussion of these issues, see Wiese (2017), Cao (2020), Facchin (2021a) and Mann and Pain (2022a).

In the Introduction to this Element, I pointed out that questions about the nature and reality of mental content constitute a significant part of the age-old mind–body problem. The trends that I have highlighted in these last sections suggest (at least to my mind) how a solution to this problem might finally emerge: not through the groundbreaking insight of a philosophical genius but through the sustained, collective effort of legions of philosophers of mind, philosophers of science and cognitive scientists.

References

Adams, Fred. 2021. "Causal Theories of Mental Content." *The Stanford Encyclopedia of Philosophy* (Fall 2021 ed.), edited by Edward Zalta. https://plato.stanford.edu/archives/fall2021/entries/content-causal/.

Adams, Fred, and Kenneth Aizawa. 1994. "Fodorian Semantics." In *Mental Representations*, edited by Stephen Stich and Ted Warfield, 223–242. Oxford: Blackwell.

Anscombe, G. E. M. 1957. *Intention*. Oxford: Basil Blackwell.

Arnellos, Argyris, and Alvaro Moreno. 2021. "Visual Perception and the Emergence of Minimal Representation." *Frontiers in Psychology* 12: 660807.

Artiga, Marc. 2016. "Liberal Representationalism: A Deflationist Defense." *dialectica* 70 (3): 407–430.

2021. "Beyond Black Dots and Nutritious Things: A Solution to the Indeterminacy Problem." *Mind and Language* 36 (3): 471–490.

Artiga, Marc, and Miguel Ángel Sebastián. 2020. "Informational Theories of Content and Mental Representation." *Review of Philosophy and Psychology* 11: 613–627.

Baker, Lynne Rudder. 1991. "Has Content Been Naturalized?" In *Meaning in Mind: Fodor and His Critics*, edited by Barry Loewer and Georges Rey, 17–32. Oxford: Blackwell.

Bauer, Mark. 2017. "Ahistorical Teleosemantics: An Alternative to Nanay." *The Southern Journal of Philosophy* 55 (2): 158–176.

Bechtel, William. 2008. *Mental Mechanisms*. New York: Psychology Press.

Beckermann, Ansgar. 1988. "Why Tropistic Systems Are Not Genuine Intentional Systems." *Erkenntnis* 29: 125–142.

Bergman, Karl. 2019. "Communities of Judgement: Towards a Teleosemantic Theory of Moral Thought and Discourse." Doctoral dissertation, Uppsala University.

2023. "Should the Teleosemanticist Be Afraid of Semantic Indeterminacy?" *Mind and Language* 38(1): 296–314.

Bermúdez, José. 2007. "What Is at Stake in the Debate on Nonconceptual Content?" *Philosophical Perspectives* 21: 55–72.

Bermúdez, José, and Arnon Cahen. 2020. "Nonconceptual Mental Content." *The Stanford Encyclopedia of Philosophy* (Summer 2020 ed.), edited by Edward Zalta. https://plato.stanford.edu/archives/sum2020/entries/content-nonconceptual/.

Block, Ned. 1978. "Troubles with Functionalism." In *Readings in the Philosophy of Psychology*, Vol. 1, edited by Ned Block, 268–305. Cambridge, MA: Harvard University Press.

1981. "Psychologism and Behaviorism." *The Philosophical Review* 90 (1): 5–43.

1986. "Advertisement for a Semantics of Psychology." In *Studies in the Philosophy of Mind* (Midwest Studies in Philosophy, Vol. 10), edited by Peter A. French, Theodore E. Uehling and Howard K. Wettstein, 615–678. Minneapolis: University of Minnesota Press.

Boghossian, Paul. 1990. "The Status of Content." *The Philosophical Review* 99 (2): 157–184.

1991. "Naturalizing Content." In *Meaning in Mind: Fodor and His Critics*, edited by Barry Loewer and Georges Rey, 65–86. Cambridge, MA: Blackwell.

Bourget, David, and Angela Mendelovici. 2019. "Phenomenal Intentionality." In *The Stanford Encyclopedia of Philosophy* (Fall 2019 ed.), edited by Edward Zalta. https://plato.stanford.edu/archives/fall2019/entries/phenomenal-intentionality/.

Braddon-Mitchell, David, and Frank Jackson. 2007. *Philosophy of Mind and Cognition* (2nd ed.). Malden, MA: Blackwell.

Brandom, Robert. 1994. *Making It Explicit*. Cambridge, MA: Harvard University Press.

Brentano, Franz. 1874/2009. *Psychology from an Empirical Standpoint*. London: Routledge.

Brown, Curtis. 2022. "Narrow Mental Content." *The Stanford Encyclopedia of Philosophy* (Summer 2022 ed.), edited by Edward Zalta. https://plato.stanford.edu/archives/sum2022/entries/content-narrow/.

Burge, Tyler. 1979. "Individualism and the Mental." In *Contemporary Perspectives in the Philosophy of Language* (Midwest Studies in Philosophy, Vol. 2), edited by Peter A. French, Theodore E. Uehling and Howard K. Wettstein, 73–121. Minneapolis: University of Minnesota Press.

2010. *Origins of Objectivity*. Oxford: Oxford University Press.

Butlin, Patrick. 2020. "Representation and the Active Consumer." *Synthese* 197: 4533–4550.

Cao, Rosa. 2020. "New Labels for Old Ideas: Predictive Processing and the Interpretation of Neural Signals." *Review of Philosophy and Psychology* 11: 517–546.

Chalmers, David. 2009. "Ontological Anti-realism." In *Metametaphysics*, edited by David Chalmers, David Manley, and Ryan Wasserman, 77–129. Oxford: Clarendon Press.

Chemero, Anthony. 2009. *Radical Embodied Cognitive Science*. Cambridge, MA: MIT Press.

Churchland, Patricia S., and Paul M. Churchland. 1983. "Stalking the Wild Epistemic Engine." *Noûs* 17 (1): 5–18.

Churchland, Paul. 2001/2007. "Neurosemantics: Of the Mapping of Minds and the Portrayal of Worlds." In *Neurophilosophy at Work*, edited by Paul Churchland, 126–160. Cambridge: Cambridge University Press.

2012. *Plato's Camera*. Cambridge, MA: MIT Press.

Clark, Andy. 2016. *Surfing Uncertainty*. Oxford: Oxford University Press.

Cochrane, Tom. 2018. *The Emotional Mind*. Cambridge: Cambridge University Press.

Coelho Mollo, Dimitri. 2022. "Deflationary Realism: Representation and Idealisation in Cognitive Science." *Mind and Language* 37: 1048–1066.

Crane, Tim. 1998. "Intentionality As the Mark of the Mental." *Royal Institute of Philosophy Supplement* 43: 229–251.

Cresswell, M. J. 1985. *Structured Meanings*. Cambridge, MA: MIT Press.

Crowther, T. M. 2006. "Two Conceptions of Conceptualism and Nonconceptualism." *Erkenntnis* 65: 245–276.

Cummins, Robert. 1989. *Meaning and Mental Representation*. Cambridge, MA: MIT Press.

1996. *Representations, Targets, and Attitudes*. Cambridge, MA: MIT Press.

Davidson, Donald. 1984. *Inquiries into Truth and Interpretation*. Oxford: Oxford University Press.

1987. "Knowing One's Own Mind." *Proceedings and Addresses of the American Philosophical Association* 60 (3): 441–458.

Dennett, Daniel. 1971. "Intentional Systems." *Journal of Philosophy* 68 (4): 87–106.

1981/1987. "True Believers." In *The Intentional Stance*, 14–42. Cambridge, MA: MIT Press.

1988/1997. "Quining Qualia." In *The Nature of Consciousness*, edited by Ned Block, Owen Flanagan and Güven Güzeldere, 619–642. Cambridge, MA: MIT Press.

de Souza Filho, Sergio. 2022. "A Dual Proposal of Minimal Conditions for Intentionality." *Synthese* 200: 115.

1991/1998. "Real Patterns." In *Brainchildren*, 95–120. Cambridge, MA: MIT Press.

2009. "Intentional Systems Theory." In *The Oxford Handbook of Philosophy of Mind*, edited by Brian McLaughlin, Ansgar Beckermann and Sven Walter, 339–350. Oxford: Oxford University Press.

Dretske, Fred. 1981. *Knowledge and the Flow of Information*. Cambridge, MA: MIT Press.

1983. "Author's Response: Why Information?" *The Behavioral and Brain Sciences* 6: 82–90.

1986. "Misrepresentation." In *Belief*, edited by Radu J. Bogdan, 17–36. Oxford: Oxford University Press.

1988. *Explaining Behavior*. Cambridge, MA: MIT Press.

1995. *Naturalizing the Mind*. Cambridge, MA: MIT Press.

Egan, Frances. 2014. "How to Think about Mental Content." *Philosophical Studies* 170: 115–135.

2022. "The Elusive Role of Normal-Proper Function in Cognitive Science." *Philosophy and Phenomenological Research* 105 (2): 468–475.

Eliasmith, Chris. 2005. "Neurosemantics and Categories." In *Handbook of Categorization in Cognitive Science*, edited by Henri Cohen and Claire Lefebvre, 1035–1054. Amsterdam: Elsevier.

2013. *How to Build a Brain*. Oxford: Oxford University Press.

Evans, Gareth. 1982. *The Varieties of Reference*. Oxford: Clarendon Press.

Facchin, Marco. 2021a. "Predictive Processing and Anti-representationalism." *Synthese* 199: 11609–11642.

2021b. "Structural Representations Do Not Meet the Job Description Challenge." *Synthese* 199: 5479–5508.

Field, Hartry. 1977. "Logic, Meaning and Conceptual Role." *Journal of Philosophy* 69 (7): 379–409.

1978. "Mental Representation." *Erkenntnis* 13: 9–61.

Fodor, Jerry. 1975. *The Language of Thought*. Cambridge, MA: MIT Press.

1984/1990. "Semantics, Wisconsin Style." In *A Theory of Content and Other Essays*, 31–49. Cambridge, MA: MIT Press.

1985/1990. "Fodor's Guide to Mental Representation: The Intelligent Auntie's Vade-Mecum." In *Mental Content and Other Essays*, 3–29. Cambridge, MA: MIT Press.

1987. *Psychosemantics*. Cambridge, MA: MIT Press.

1990a. "A Theory of Content, I: The Problem." In *A Theory of Content and Other Essays*, 51–87. Cambridge, MA: MIT Press.

1990b. "A Theory of Content, II: The Theory." In *A Theory of Content and Other Essays*, 89–136. Cambridge, MA: MIT Press.

1991. "Replies." In *Meaning in Mind: Fodor and His Critics*, edited by Barry Loewer and Georges Rey, 255–319. Oxford: Blackwell.

Fodor, Jerry, and Zenon Pylyshyn. 2015. *Mind without Meanings*. Cambridge, MA: MIT Press.

Frankish, Keith. 2016. "Illusionism As a Theory of Consciousness." *Journal of Consciousness Studies* 23 (11–12): 11–39.

Frege, Gottlob. 1892/1994a. "Über Sinn und Bedeutung." In *Funktion, Begriff, Bedeutung*, 40–65. Göttingen: Vandenhoeck & Ruprecht.

1892/1994b. "Über Begriff und Gegenstand." In *Funktion, Begriff, Bedeutung*, 66–80. Göttingen: Vandenhoeck & Ruprecht.

Fresco, Nir. 2021. "Information, Cognition, and Objectivity." *American Philosophical Quarterly* 58 (3): 251–267.

Fresco, Nir, Simona Ginsburg and Eva Jablonka. 2020. "Functional Information: A Graded Taxonomy of Difference Makers." *Review of Philosophy and Psychology* 11: 547–567.

Gallistel, C. R., and Adam Philip King. 2010. *Memory and the Computational Brain*. Malden, MA: Wiley-Blackwell.

Ganson, Todd. 2020. "A Role for Representations in Inflexible Behavior." *Biology and Philosophy* 35: 1–18.

2021. "An Alternative to the Causal Theory of Perception." *Australasian Journal of Philosophy* 99 (4): 683–695.

Garson, Justin. 2017. "A Generalized Selected Effects Theory of Function." 84: 523–543.

2019a. *What Biological Functions Are and Why They Matter*. Cambridge: Cambridge University Press.

2019b. "Do Constancy Mechanisms Save Distal Contents?" *The Philosophical Quarterly* 69 (275): 409–417.

2022. "Response to Neander's Critics." *Philosophy and Phenomenological Research* 105 (2): 490–503.

Gladziejewski, Pawel. 2016. "Predictive Coding and Representationalism." *Synthese* 193: 559–582.

Gladziejewski, Pawel, and Marcin Milkowski. 2017. "Structural Representations: Causally Relevant and Different from Detectors." *Biology and Philosophy* 32: 337–355.

Glock, Hans-Johann. 2015. "Propositional Attitudes, Intentional Content and Other Representationalist Myths." In *Mind, Language and Action*, edited by Danièle Moyal-Sharrock, Volker Munz and Annalisa Coliva, 512–537. Berlin: De Gruyter.

Godfrey-Smith, Peter. 1989. "Misinformation." *Canadian Journal of Philosophy* 19 (4): 533–550.

1994. "A Modern History Theory of Functions." *Noûs* 28 (3): 344–362.

2006. "Mental Representation, Naturalism and Teleosemantics." In *Teleosemantics*, edited by Graham Macdonald and David Papineau, 42–68. Oxford: Oxford University Press.

Graham, George, Terence Horgan and John Tienson. 2017. "Consciousness and Intentionality." In *The Blackwell Companion to Consciousness* (2nd ed.), edited by Susan Schneider and Max Velmans, 519–535. Malden, MA: Wiley-Blackwell.

Green, E. J. 2017. "Psychosemantics and the Rich/Thin Debate." *Philosophical Perspectives* 31: 153–186.

Greenberg, Mark. 2006. Setting Asymmetric Dependence Straight. *UCLA Public Law & Legal Theory Series*. https://escholarship.org/uc/item/92z5q0sd.

Grice, Paul. 1957. "Meaning." *The Philosophical Review* 66 (3): 377–388.

Harman, Gilbert. 1982. "Conceptual Role Semantics." *Notre Dame Journal of Formal Logic* 23 (2): 242–256.

Heck, Richard. 2000. "Nonconceptual Content and the 'Space of Reasons'." *Philosophical Review* 109 (4): 483–523.

Hill, Christopher S. 2022. "Neander on a Mark of the Mental." *Philosophy and Phenomenological Research* 105 (2): 484–489.

Hofweber, Thomas. 2005. "A Puzzle about Ontology." *Noûs* 39 (2): 256–283.

Hohwy, Jakob. 2013. *The Predictive Mind*. Oxford: Oxford University Press.

Horgan, Terence, and George Graham. 2012. "Phenomenal Intentionality and Content Determinacy." In *Prospects for Meaning*, edited by Richard Schantz, 321–344. Berlin: De Gruyter.

Horgan, Terence, and John Tienson. 2002. "The Intentionality of Phenomenology and the Phenomenology of Intentionality." In *Philosophy of Mind: Classical and Contemporary Readings*, edited by David Chalmers, 520–533. Oxford: Oxford University Press.

Hundertmark, Fabian. 2018. "Mind and Function: Teleosemantics beyond Selected Effects." PhD dissertation, Bielefeld University.

2021. "Explaining How to Perceive the New: Causal-Informational Teleosemantics and Productive Response Functions." *Synthese* 198: 5335–5350.

Hutto, Daniel, and Erik Myin. 2013. *Radicalizing Enactivism*. Cambridge, MA: MIT Press.

2017. *Evolving Enactivism*. Cambridge, MA: MIT Press.

Hutto, Daniel, and Glenda Satne. 2015. "The Natural Origins of Content." *Philosophia* 43: 521–536.

Jackson, Frank. 1998. *From Metaphysics to Ethics*. Oxford: Clarendon Press.

Jacob, Pierre. 1997. *What Minds Can Do*. Cambridge: Cambridge University Press.

Kelly, S. D. 2001. "Demonstrative Concepts and Experience." *The Philosophical Review* 110 (3): 397–420.

Kiefer, Alex, and Jakob Hohwy. 2018. "Content and Misrepresentation in Hierarchical Generative Models." *Synthese* 195: 2387–2415.

King, Jeffrey C. 2007. *The Nature and Structure of Content*. Oxford: Oxford University Press.

Kirchhoff, Michael, and Ian Robertson. 2018. "Enactivism and Predictive Processing: A Non-Representational View." *Philosophical Explorations* 21 (2): 264–281.

Kriegel, Uriah. 2018. *Brentano's Philosophical System*. Oxford: Oxford University Press.

Kripke, Saul. 1980. *Naming and Necessity*. Cambridge, MA: Harvard University Press.

1982. *Wittgenstein on Rules and Private Language*. Oxford: Blackwell.

Lee, Jonny. 2019. "Structural Representations and Two Problems of Content." *Mind and Language* 34 (5): 606–626.

Lewis, David. 1972. "General Semantics." In *Semantics in Natural Language*, edited by Donald Davidson and Gilbert Harman, 169–218. Dordrecht: Reidel.

1974. "Radical Interpretation." *Synthese* 27: 331–344.

Lloyd, Dan. 1989. *Simple Minds*. Cambridge, MA: MIT Press.

Loar, Brian. 2003. "Phenomenal Intentionality As the Basis of Mental Content." In *Reflections and Replies: Essays on the Philosophy of Tyler Burge*, edited by Martin Hahn and B. Ramberg, 229–258. Cambridge, MA: MIT Press.

Loewer, Barry. 1983. "Information and Belief." *The Behavioral and Brain Sciences* 6: 75–76.

2017. "A Guide to Naturalizing Semantics." In *A Companion to the Philosophy of Language* (2nd ed.), edited by Bob Hale, Alexander Miller and Crispin Wright, 174–190. Malden, MA: Wiley-Blackwell.

Mann, Stephen, and Ross Pain. 2022a. "Teleosemantics and the Free Energy Principle." *Biology and Philosophy* 37: 34.

2022b. "Teleosemantics and the Hard Problem of Content." *Philosophical Psychology* 35 (1): 22–46.

Martínez, Manolo. 2011. "Imperative Content and the Painfulness of Pain." *Phenomenology and the Cognitive Sciences* 10: 67–90.

2013. "Teleosemantics and Indeterminacy." *dialectica* 67 (4): 427–453.

2019. "Representations Are Rate-Distortion Sweet Spots." *Philosophy of Science* 86: 1214–1226.

Matthen, Mohan. 1988. "Biological Functions and Perceptual Content." *The Journal of Philosophy* 85 (1): 5–27.

McDowell, John. 1994. *Mind and World*. Cambridge, MA: Harvard University Press.

McGinn, Colin. 1996. *The Character of Mind* (2nd ed.). Oxford: Oxford University Press.

McGrath, Matthew, and Devin Frank. 2020. "Propositions." *The Stanford Encyclopedia of Philosophy (*Winter 2020 ed.), edited by Edward Zalta. https://plato.stanford.edu/archives/win2020/entries/propositions/.

Mendelovici, Angela. 2018. *The Phenomal Basis of Intentionality.* Oxford: Oxford University Press.

Mendola, Joseph. 2003. "A Dilemma for Asymmetric Dependence." *Noûs* 37 (2): 232–257.

Milkowski, Marcin. 2015. "The Hard Problem of Content: Solved (Long Ago)." *Studies in Logic, Grammar and Rhetoric* 41 (54): 73–88.

Millikan, Ruth. 1984. *Language, Thought, and Other Biological Categories.* Cambridge, MA: MIT Press.

1989. "Biosemantics." *The Journal of Philosophy* 86 (6): 281–297.

1991. "Speaking Up for Darwin." In *Meaning in Mind: Fodor and His Critics*, edited by Barry Loewer and Georges Rey, 151–165. Cambridge, MA: Blackwell.

1996. "On Swampkinds." *Mind and Language* 11 (1): 103–117.

2004. *Varieties of Meaning.* Cambridge, MA: MIT Press.

2013. "Reply to Neander." In *Millikan and Her Critics*, edited by Dan Ryder, Justine Kingsbury and Ken Williford, 37–40. Malden, MA: Wiley-Blackwell.

2017. *Beyond Concepts.* Oxford: Oxford University Press.

2021. "Neuroscience and Teleosemantics." *Synthese* 199: 2457–2465.

Morgan, Alex. 2014. "Representations Gone Mental." *Synthese* 191: 213–244.

Nanay, Bence. 2014. "Teleosemantics without Etiology." *Philosophy of Science* 81 (5): 798–810.

Neander, Karen. 1991. "Functions As Selected Effects." *Philosophy of Science* 58 (2): 168–184.

1995. "Malfunctioning and Misrepresenting." *Philosophical Studies* 79: 109–141.

1996. "Swampman Meets Swampcow." *Mind and Language* 11 (1): 118–129.

2006. "Content for Cognitive Science." In *Teleosemantics*, edited by Graham Macdonald and David Papineau, 167–194. Oxford: Oxford University Press.

2013. "Toward an Informational Teleosemantics." In *Millikan and Her Critics*, edited by Justine Kingsbury, Dan Ryder and Kenneth Williford, 21–36. Malden, MA: Wiley-Blackwell.

2017. *A Mark of the Mental.* Cambridge, MA: MIT Press.

Nimtz, Christian. 2017. "Two-Dimensional Semantics." In *The Blackwell Companion to the Philosophy of Language*, edited by Bob Hale, Crispin Wright and Alex Miller, 948–970. Oxford: Blackwell.

Nirshberg, Gregory, and Lawrence Shapiro. 2021. "Structural and Indicator Representations: A Difference in Degree, not Kind." *Synthese* 198: 7647–7664.

O'Brien, Gerard. 2015. "How Does Mind Matter? Solving the Content Causation Problem." In *Open MIND*, edited by Thomas Metzinger and Jennifer M. Windt, 1–14. Frankfurt: MIND Group.

O'Brien, Gerard, and Jon Opie. 2004. "Notes Toward a Structuralist Theory of Mental Representation." In *Representation in Mind*, edited by H. Clapin, P. Staines and P. Slezak, 1–20. Amsterdam: Elsevier.

Orlandi, Nico. 2020. "Representing As Coordinating with Absence." In *What Are Mental Representations?*, edited by Joulia Smortchkova, Krzysztof Dolega and Tobias Schlicht, 101–134. Oxford: Oxford University Press.

Papineau, David. 1984. "Representation and Explanations." *Philosophy of Science* 51 (4): 550–572.

1993. *Philosophical Naturalism*. Oxford: Basil Blackwell.

1998. "Teleosemantics and Indeterminacy." *Australasian Journal of Philosophy* 76 (1): 1–14.

2001. "The Status of Teleosemantics, or How to Stop Worrying About Swampman." *Australasian Journal of Philosophy* 79 (2): 279–289.

2021. *The Metaphysics of Sensory Experience*. Oxford: Oxford University Press.

2022. "Swampman, Teleosemantics and Kind Essences." *Synthese* 200: 509. https://doi.org/https://doi.org/10.1007/s11229-022-03966-7.

Pavese, Carlotta. 2017. "A Theory of Practical Meaning." *Philosophical Topics* 45 (2): 65–96.

Peacocke, Christopher. 1992. *A Study of Concepts*. Cambridge, MA: MIT Press.

Piccinini, Gualtiero. 2020. *Neurocognitive Mechanisms*. Oxford: Oxford University Press.

2022. "Situated Neural Representations: Solving the Problems of Content." *Frontiers in Neurobiotics* 16: 1–13.

Pietroski, Paul. 1992. "Intentional and Teleological Error." *Pacific Philosophical Quarterly* 73: 267–281.

Platts, Mark. 1979. *Ways of Meaning*. London: Routledge and Kegan Paul.

Price, Carolyn. 2001. *Functions in Mind*. Oxford: Clarendon Press.

Prinz, Jesse. 2000. "The Duality of Content." *Philosophical Studies* 100: 1–34.

2002. *Furnishing the Mind*. Cambridge, MA: MIT Press.

Putnam, Hilary. 1975. "The Meaning of 'Meaning'." In *Language, Mind and Knowledge*, edited by Keith Gunderson, 131–193. Minneapolis: University of Minnesota Press.

Quine, W. V. O. 1960. *Word and Object*. Cambridge, MA: MIT Press.

Ramsey, William. 2007. *Representation Reconsidered*. Cambridge: Cambridge University Press.

Rescorla, Michael. 2013. "Millikan on Honeybee Navigation and Communication." In *Millikan and Her Critics*, edited by Justine Kingsbury, Dan Ryder and Kenneth Williford, 87–102. Malden, MA: Wiley-Blackwell.

Roche, William, and Elliott Sober. 2021. "Disjunction and Distality: The Hard Problem for Pure Probabilistic Causal Theories of Mental Content." *Synthese* 198: 7197–7230.

Rosenberg, Alexander. 2014. "Disenchanted Naturalism." In *Contemporary Philosophical Naturalism and Its Implications*, edited by Bana Bashour and Hans D. Muller, 17–36. New York: Routledge.

Rupert, Robert. 1999. "The Best Test Theory of Extension: First Principle(s)." *Mind and Language* 14 (3): 321–355.

2008. "Causal Theories of Mental Content." *Philosophy Compass* 3 (2): 353–380.

2018. "Representation and Mental Representation." *Philosophical Explorations* 21 (2): 204–225.

Russell, Bertrand. 1903. *Principles of Mathematics* (2nd ed.). New York: Norton.

1918/1985. *The Philosophy of Logical Atomism*. Chicago, IL: Open Court.

Ryder, Dan. 2004. "SINBAD Neurosemantics: A Theory of Mental Representation." *Mind and Language* 19 (2): 211–240.

Salmon, Nathan. 1986. *Frege's Puzzle*. Cambridge, MA: MIT Press.

Scarantino, Andrea. 2015. "Information As a Probabilistic Difference Maker." *Australasian Journal of Philosophy* 93 (3): 419–443.

Schmidt, Eva. 2015. *Modest Nonconceptualism*. Cham: Springer.

Schulte, Peter. 2012. "How Frogs See the World: Putting Millikan's Teleosemantics to the Test." *Philosophia* 40 (3): 483–496.

2015. "Perceptual Representations: A Teleosemantic Answer to the Breadth-of-Application Problem." *Biology and Philosophy* 30 (1): 119–136.

2018. "Perceiving the World Outside: How to Solve the Distality Problem for Informational Teleosemantics." *Philosophical Quarterly* 68 (271): 349–369.

2019a. "Challenging Liberal Representationalism: A Reply to Artiga." *dialectica* 73 (3): 331–348.

2019b. "Naturalizing the Content of Desire." *Philosophical Studies* 176 (1): 161–174.

2020. "Why Mental Content Is Not Like Water: Reconsidering the Reductive Claims of Teleosemantics." *Synthese* 197: 2271–2290.

2021. "The Nature of Perceptual Constancies." *Philosophy and Phenomenological Research* 103 (1): 3–20.

2022. "Constancy Mechanisms and Distal Content: A Reply to Garson." *Philosophical Quarterly* 72 (1): 229–237.

Schulte, Peter, and Karen Neander. 2022. "Teleological Theories of Mental Content." *The Stanford Encyclopedia of Philosophy* (Summer 2022 ed.), edited by Edward Zalta. https://plato.stanford.edu/archives/sum2022/entries/content-teleological/.

Searle, John. 1983. *Intentionality*. Cambridge: Cambridge University Press.

Segal, Gabriel. 2000. *A Slim Book about Narrow Content*. Cambridge, MA: MIT Press.

Shagrir, Oron. 2001. "Content, Computation and Externalism." *Mind* 110 (438): 368–400.

Shannon, Claude E. 1948. "A Mathematical Theory of Communication." *The Bell System Technical Journal* 27 (3): 379–423.

Shea, Nicholas. 2007. "Consumers Need Information: Supplementing Teleosemantics with an Input Condition." *Philosophy and Phenomenological Research* 75 (2): 404–435.

2013. "Millikan's Isomorphism Requirement." In *Millikan and Her Critics*, edited by Dan Ryder, Justine Kingsbury and Kenneth Williford, 63–80. Malden, MA: Wiley-Blackwell.

2018. *Representation in Cognitive Science*. Oxford: Oxford University Press.

Soames, Scott. 1987. "Direct Reference, Propositional Attitudes and Semantic Content." *Philosophical Topics* 15 (1): 47–87.

2010. *What Is Meaning?* Princeton, NJ: Princeton University Press.

Sosa, Ernest. 1983. "One the 'Content' and 'Relevance' of Information-Theoretic Epistemology." *The Behavioral and Brain Sciences* 6: 79–81.

Sprevak, Mark. 2013. "Fictionalism about Neural Representation." *The Monist* 96 (4): 539–560.

Stalnaker, Robert. 1976. "Propositions." In *Issues in the Philosophy of Language*, edited by Alfred F. MacKay and Daniel D. Merrill, 79–91. New Haven, CT: Yale University Press.

Stampe, Dennis. 1977. "Toward a Causal Theory of Linguistic Representation." In *Studies in the Philosophy of Language*. Midwest Studies in Philosophy: Vol. 2, edited by Peter A. French, Theodore E. Uehling and Howard K. Wettstein, 81–102. Minneapolis: University of Minnesota Press.

Sterelny, Kim. 1990. *The Representational Theory of Mind*. Oxford: Blackwell.

1995. "Basic Minds." *Philosophical Perspectives* 9: 251–270.

Stich, Stephen. 1983. *From Folk Psychology to Cognitive Science*. Cambridge, MA: MIT Press.

Strawson, Galen. 2008. "Real Intentionality 3: Why Intentionality Entails Consciousness." In *Real Materialism and Other Essays*, 53–74. Oxford: Oxford University Press.

Swoyer, Chris. 1991. "Structural Representation and Surrogative Reasoning." *Synthese* 87: 449–508.

Tye, Michael. 1995. *Ten Problems of Consciousness*. Cambridge, MA: MIT Press.

2006. "Nonconceptual Content, Richness, and Fineness of Grain." In *Perceptual Experience*, edited by Tamar Gendler Szabo and John Hawthorne, 504–530. Oxford: Oxford University Press.

Usher, Marius. 2001. "A Statistical Referential Theory of Content: Using Information Theory to Account for Misrepresentation." *Mind and Language* 16 (3): 311–334.

van Gelder, Tim. 1995. "What Might Cognition Be, If Not Computation?" *Journal of Philosophy* 92 (7): 345–381.

Vos, I. A., C. M. J. Pieterse, and S. C. M. van Wees. 2013. "Costs and Benefits of Hormone-Regulated Plant Defenses." *Plant Pathology* 1: 43–55.

Whiting, Daniel. 2022. "Conceptual Role Semantics." *Internet Encyclopedia of Philosophy*. https://iep.utm.edu/conceptual-role-semantics/.

Wiese, Wanja. 2017. "What Are the Contents of Representations in Predictive Processing?" *Phenomenology and the Cognitive Sciences* 16 (4): 715–736.

Wiese, Wanja, and Thomas Metzinger. 2017. "Vanilla PP for Philosophers: A Primer on Predictive Processing." In *Philosophy and Predictive Processing*, edited by Thomas Metzinger and Wanja Wiese, 1–18. Frankfurt: MIND Group.

Wittgenstein, Ludwig. 1921/2003. *Tractatus Logico-Philosophicus*. Frankfurt: Suhrkamp.

Yli-Vakkuri, Juhani, and John Hawthorne. 2018. *Narrow Content*. Oxford: Oxford University Press.

Acknowledgments

I would like to thank Hannah Altehenger, Marc Artiga, Keith Frankish, Frank Hofmann, Fabian Hundertmark, Caroline Stankozi, Adrian Wieczorek and two anonymous referees for Cambridge University Press for their insightful comments and suggestions, which greatly helped to improve this Element.

Cambridge Elements =

Philosophy of Mind

Keith Frankish

The University of Sheffield

Keith Frankish is a philosopher specializing in philosophy of mind, philosophy of psychology, and philosophy of cognitive science. He is the author of *Mind and Supermind* (Cambridge University Press, 2004) and *Consciousness* (2005), and has also edited or coedited several collections of essays, including *The Cambridge Handbook of Cognitive Science* (Cambridge University Press, 2012), *The Cambridge Handbook of Artificial Intelligence* (Cambridge University Press, 2014) (both with William Ramsey), and *Illusionism as a Theory of Consciousness* (2017).

About the Series

This series provides concise, authoritative introductions to contemporary work in philosophy of mind, written by leading researchers and including both established and emerging topics. It provides an entry point to the primary literature and will be the standard resource for researchers, students, and anyone wanting a firm grounding in this fascinating field.

Cambridge Elements ≡

Philosophy of Mind

Elements in the Series

Mindreading and Social Cognition
Jane Suilin Lavelle

Free Will
Derk Pereboom

Philosophy of Neuroscience
William Bechtel and Linus Ta-Lun Huang

The Metaphysics of Mind
Janet Levin

Mental Illness
Tim Thornton

Imagination and Creative Thinking
Amy Kind

Attention and Mental Control
Carolyn Dicey Jennings

Biological Cognition
Bryce Huebner and Jay Schulkin

Embodied and Enactive Approaches to Cognition
Shaun Gallagher

Mental Content
Peter Schulte

A full series listing is available at: www.cambridge.org/EPMI

Printed in the United States
by Baker & Taylor Publisher Services